DOING THE RIGHT THING

ALSO BY THE SAME AUTHOR

Tata Log: Eight Modern Stories from a Timeless Institution
The Curious Marketer: Expeditions in Branding and Consumer Behaviour
An Extreme Love of Coffee: A Novel
#Tata Stories: 40 Timeless Tales to Inspire You
Office Secrets: 50 Human Truths You Should Absolutely Know
Restless Lives
Jamsetji Tata: Powerful Learnings for Corporate Success

DOING THE RIGHT THING
LEARNINGS FROM
RATAN TATA

HARISH BHAT

PENGUIN
BUSINESS
An imprint of Penguin Random House

PENGUIN BUSINESS

Penguin Business is an imprint of the Penguin Random House group of companies whose addresses can be found at global.penguinrandomhouse.com

Published by Penguin Random House India Pvt. Ltd
4th Floor, Capital Tower 1, MG Road,
Gurugram 122 002, Haryana, India

Penguin Random House India

First published in Penguin Business by Penguin Random House India 2025

10 9 8 7 6 5 4 3

ISBN 9780143479857

Typeset in Sabon Lt Pro by MAP Systems, Bengaluru, India
Printed at Thomson Press India Private Limited

www.penguin.co.in

This book is inspired by Ratan Tata.

I dedicate it to his memory.

This book is not a comprehensive chronicle of his life. It is not a biography. It is not an objective analysis of his legacy.

This is a simple book that focuses on why and how Ratan Tata always endeavoured to do the right thing. In these pages, you will find some lovely Ratan Tata stories that can inspire each of us, and a few lessons from his life that can help us do the right thing ourselves.

Contents

Preface

A Question About Ratan Tata

On the morning of 10 October 2024, a long and winding queue began forming outside the gates of the National Centre for the Performing Arts (NCPA) in Mumbai. Tens of thousands of men and women, young and old, had reached there, travelling long distances, for their last glimpse of a man whom they admired, adored and loved.

That man was Ratan Tata. He had passed away the previous night at the age of eighty-six years. His body was now being brought to the lawns of the NCPA, where the public could pay their homage.

I too had taken an early morning flight from my home town in Bangalore to pay my last respects to the man whose life and actions had impacted me profoundly. I was unable to sleep well the previous night after I heard about Ratan Tata's passing. Now, at the NCPA, as I passed by his body which lay in a glass coffin, I closed my eyes and offered my prayers. Then, I stood back on one side, wanting to spend some time close to the man who would soon be taken away from us forever.

I prayed that the departed soul would rest in peace, and then thanked him for leading the Tata group from strength to strength, whilst ensuring its values were carefully protected and nurtured. I thanked him for dedicating his life to the nation and to the Tatas, and for being a role model from whom so many of us took inspiration. At a personal level, I thanked him for giving me a wonderful professional home for nearly four decades.

I joined the Tata group in 1987 at the age of twenty-five, and here I am today, at sixty-three, still happily part of the family. Ratan Tata (RNT to many of us in the Tata group) was a member of the final interview committee which had recruited me to the Tata Administrative Service. Thereafter, he had been a constant source of inspiration and reassurance throughout my life and career. Though I never worked with him directly, I had met him a few times and cherished each opportunity to speak with him.

But today, it was not just Tata people like me who experienced a deep sadness. There were millions of Indians who felt a strange sense of personal loss, even though they may never have met him or interacted with him. As people passed by his coffin, paying their respects, I could see many of them sobbing uncontrollably.

Soon, priests from many religions—Zoroastrianism, Hinduism, Islam, Buddhism, Christianity, Jainism—stood up to offer their prayers, one by one. As they recited their prayers, I kept looking at Ratan Tata, now lying so peaceful in death. Suddenly, I broke down in tears, and could not think any more. Tears came flooding out of nowhere. One of the priests saw me crying, put his arms around me and comforted me. It could well have been Ratan Tata speaking through that priest, because I think that is what RNT would have done.

Later that afternoon, the cortège left the lawns of the NCPA on its way to the Worli crematorium where the final rites would be performed. At a nearby junction, I saw that a huge crowd had gathered, and they were raising the Hindi slogan '*Ratan Tata amar rahe*' (Ratan Tata will live forever).

Meanwhile, television channels across the country were broadcasting live images from the Worli crematorium, where a state funeral had been organized. Thousands of people had gathered there too, wanting to offer their respects, and the police had a difficult time controlling the crowds.

Within a few hours, hundreds of posters appeared across the roads of Mumbai and other cities, paying homage to Ratan Tata. Newspapers ran special supplements to pay tribute to him. Every second post on social media was about him. There was an outpouring of respect and love that was both special and rare.

For instance, a young lady from Bengaluru, who reached the NCPA late and missed paying her respects to him, reached out to me over LinkedIn with an urgent message, saying, 'Harish, I am the founder of a start-up in Bangalore. By the time I landed in Mumbai and reached NCPA, Mr Tata's body had already been taken to the crematorium. I felt so disheartened, so furious with myself for not making it on time. I would at least like to go to Bombay House [headquarters of the Tata group] and see the place where Mr Ratan Tata worked out of for many years. That would be a pilgrimage for me, because he has been such a great inspiration to my daughter and me. Can you please help me with this. I know I am just trying my luck.' (Note: My colleagues and I helped obtain permission for this young lady to briefly visit the foyer of Bombay House and pay her respects to Ratan Tata there.)

A few days later, as I reflected on all these events, one question kept coming back to my mind. Why were millions of Indians impacted so deeply and so personally by Ratan Tata's passing away?

I pondered many possible answers to this question.

Could it be because Ratan Tata led the Tata group splendidly, achieving many business successes, and growing the group's revenues handsomely from $6 billion to $100 billion during his tenure of two decades as the chairman of Tata Sons?

Could it be because of the admirable philanthropy initiatives he led through the Tata Charitable Trusts, including the creation of some of India's finest cancer hospitals, and the large investments committed to the fight against COVID-19?

Could it be because of some of his personal traits—grace, humility and elegance, despite being one of the nation's most powerful men?

Could it be because his highest commitment was to give back to the nation, rather than accumulate wealth and power, which defines so many well-known business leaders today?

Perhaps all these elements have combined together in our minds to create the respect and love that we feel for Ratan Tata. But there is also one other key feature of the great man which has contributed to this deep and fond feeling that we have for him. I have spoken to many people who knew him, and they inevitably refer to his consistent desire to always do 'the right thing'.

Whether it be in business, philanthropy or in his interactions with leaders and ordinary people, 'doing the right thing' appears to have been one of the strongest drivers in Ratan Tata's life. It influenced his thoughts and actions, and perhaps led, directly or indirectly, to all the elements which have been listed above.

Particularly because this is so rare in public life, Ratan Tata has stood out as a beacon of hope and aspiration for all of us. So many of us aspire to do the right thing in our own lives. However, as human beings, we often fall prey to various temptations or choose to take our own convenient deviations. Therefore, when we see a man who stands by and does what is right at all times, we also see in him a person we wish to emulate. We would like to be inspired by him and learn from him, so that we can become the best versions of ourselves.

That is the essential thought behind this book. In these pages, I hope to explore various facets of 'doing the right thing' by examining several events in Ratan Tata's life and career. In this process of exploration, I have spoken to many people who have worked closely with him. I have also researched many of his writings and interviews. Finally, I have delved into my own reflections and observations, gathered over nearly four decades of being part of the Tata group.

Using all these inputs and drawing on many real-life stories from Ratan Tata's life, I have attempted to put together an exploration of this important subject. I would like to clarify that this book is not a biography of Ratan Tata, nor does it claim to be a comprehensive or objective review of his life. The stories I have narrated in this book are merely the stories from his life that have appealed most to me, and which help us explore what 'doing the right thing' meant to him.

I hope you will find the chapters that follow interesting and inspirational. Most importantly, I hope this book will guide each of us in doing the right thing in our own lives.

1

Ratan Tata: Life and Career

Before we delve into the subject of 'doing the right thing', an important context to bear in mind would be the life and career of the protagonist, Ratan Tata. Glimpses into the trajectory of his life may give us some understanding of how his values were moulded and where his thinking evolved.

Early Years

Ratan Tata was born in Mumbai on 28 December 1937 to Soonoo and Naval Tata. His father, Naval Tata, was the adopted son of Ratanji Tata, the younger son of Jamsetji Tata, who founded the Tata group.

Ratan's was a household that was steeped in Tata tradition. There would also have been great pride in belonging to the family of Jamsetji Tata, who was and continues to be regarded as the father of modern Indian industry.

When Ratan was ten years of age, his parents separated. Subsequently, both his father and his mother had second marriages. From around the time of their separation, Ratan came under the care of his paternal grandmother, Lady Navajbai Tata. She was a disciplinarian with a firm sense of values. Ratan was raised by her, and grew up under her strict but benevolent eyes.

1950s: Schooling and Education

Ratan Tata's initial schooling was at the Campion School in Mumbai, and thereafter at the Cathedral and John Connon School in Mumbai and the Bishop Cotton School in Shimla. In 1955, he left for Cornell University at Ithaca in New York, USA. Cornell is one of the great universities of the world, and this is where Ratan pursued his studies in architecture and structural engineering.

The choice of subjects is interesting. Ratan initially studied engineering at Cornell, in deference to his father's wishes. Later, he took courage and changed his course of studies to architecture, which he loved. Eventually, he would complete his studies in both disciplines within seven years. During these years (1955–62), he also travelled across the USA extensively and was influenced greatly by the technological progress that he saw in that country. He was so enamoured by California that he considered living the rest of his life there. In fact, he worked briefly at an architecture firm in Los Angeles.

1960s: Return to India

Around the time of Ratan's graduation in 1962, his grandmother Navajbai Tata fell ill. Navajbai was the grand old matriarch of the Tata family then, and Ratan was forced to return to India. He had in hand a job offer from IBM. However, J.R.D. Tata, who was chairman of the Tata group at that time, persuaded Ratan to join the Tatas.

Ratan Tata's career in the Tata group thus began in the year 1962, as an assistant in Tata Industries in Mumbai. Later that year, he spent six months as an intern at the Jamshedpur factory of Tata Motors (then called TELCO)—this company would, in later years, become his first love. By 1963, he had moved to Tata Steel (then called TISCO), also in Jamshedpur, as a trainee.

For the next few years, Ratan Tata lived and worked in Jamshedpur, the town named after his great-grandfather,

Jamsetji Tata. In this town, which is managed by the Tata group and steeped in Tata tradition, Ratan Tata cut his professional teeth. In 1965, he was appointed technical officer in TISCO's engineering division. Four years later, he took up a role as the Tata group's resident representative in Australia.

1970s: The Years at NELCO

In 1971, Ratan Tata was appointed to his first major independent leadership role in the Tata group. He was named director-in-charge of the National Radio and Electronics Company, also known as NELCO. The company was struggling when he took charge. Ratan navigated several challenges expertly to make the organization profitable and it also grew its market share significantly. The company had to manage several issues and not all of Ratan's dreams for NELCO could come true. At NELCO, he also faced the first big industrial relations dispute of his career. He displayed his mettle in handling the lockout firmly and bringing the matter to a good and fair conclusion.

During the 1970s, Ratan was also charged with the task of saving Empress Mills, the first greenfield enterprise of the Tata group, located in Nagpur. These textile mills were in poor financial condition when he took charge. Under Ratan's leadership, the company soon became profitable. However, a few years later, it ran into a tough patch that impacted the entire textile industry across India and began incurring losses. His plans for the long-term revival of the mills could not eventually be implemented because, in the mid-1980s, Tata Sons refused to provide further funds that were urgently required, ahead of a full-fledged rehabilitation effort. In particular, one of the senior directors of Tata Sons, the noted constitutional lawyer and tax expert Nani Palkhivala, took a stance that the proposed rehabilitation plan was not viable.

In 1974, Ratan Tata was appointed to the board of Tata Sons, the holding company of the Tata group, as a director. In May 1978, he sent a confidential note to J.R.D. Tata, urging him to initiate the development of a strategic plan for the Tata group, addressing issues of growth and earnings, but also, most importantly, how the Tatas should operate in the future.

1980s: Leading Tata Industries

In September 1981, Ratan Tata was appointed the chairman of Tata Industries. At that time, Tata Industries was a company in search of a new mission. Ratan Tata took up this position with great energy and focus and applied his mind to transforming the company.

He soon arrived at the conclusion that this company could lead the Tata group's forays into high-technology businesses, promoting and incubating them for the future. These would, by their nature, be relatively high-risk businesses but if they succeeded they could open entirely new horizons for the group.

These and other related thoughts came together in the Tata strategic plan, which Ratan Tata authored in 1983. During this time, his mother had fallen seriously unwell with cancer and was under treatment in a hospital in New York City. Despite the demands of work, Ratan travelled to the USA and spent time with her, multitasking with his official responsibilities all the while. Much of the strategic plan was drafted at her bedside.

The Tata strategic plan laid out a clear blueprint for the group's future, including new businesses that could be promoted by Tata Industries as well as new areas that existing large Tata companies could foray into. But the plan did not make much progress, particularly with respect to existing companies. R.M. Lala refers specifically to this in his book *The Creation of Wealth*: 'The plan was stymied because of resistance from the powerful chief executives of some individual Tata companies, who saw the younger Tata's effort as an intrusion into their own turf.'

Notwithstanding this situation, Ratan Tata moved forward, envisioning many high-technology businesses under the umbrella of Tata Industries, the company which he was leading. Over the next several years, a number of companies would blossom out of this approach, including Tata IBM, Tata Elxsi, Tata Honeywell and Tata Auto Components (TACO). In promoting these ventures, Ratan Tata not only created new growth avenues, but also brought a new-age technology mindset into the group.

1990s: Initial Years as Chairman of Tata Sons

On 23 March 1991, J.R.D. Tata informed Ratan Tata that he had decided to retire and wanted to appoint Ratan as the chairman of Tata Sons. Two days later, Ratan took charge as chairman of Tata Sons and Tata Trusts. He had just assumed the mantle of leading India's largest private sector corporate entity.

Ratan soon applied himself to the task which he believed was both urgent and essential: restructuring the Tata organization which, in his view, was then operating as 'diverse fragments under a single name'. His objective was to ensure that the Tatas operated as a unified group with a coherent direction and also to make the group globally competitive for the future while remaining true to the values which had always defined its essence.

Quite coincidentally, 1991 also saw the launch of India's economic liberalization, so Ratan Tata had to shape the group for a very different competitive era. This had to be done with great urgency, because restrictions on industry, licensing and the entry of global competition had been largely eliminated by the Indian government in one fell swoop.

Ratan Tata moved forward with several transformative processes within his first few years as chairman.

First, he established the right to manage companies of the group by raising the equity stake held by Tata Sons in large companies of the group to at least 26 per cent. This compared to single-digit equity holdings of the past—for instance, prior to this move, Tata Sons' equity holding in Tata Power was around 4 per cent, and in Tata Steel around 8 per cent, putting them at the risk of hostile acquisitions.

Second, he introduced a unified Tata brand logo, which would be used uniformly by all Tata companies, under a licence from Tata Sons. This licence, housed within a well-structured 'Brand Equity and Business Promotion (BEBP)' agreement, specified several requirements that companies had to meet to earn the right to use the Tata name.

Third, he identified seven core business sectors that the Tata group would focus on, leading to focused investments in these sectors and divestments in some other segments.

Fourth, he emphasized financial performance—both growth and profitability—while simultaneously launching a group-wide push for the highest levels of quality and overall business excellence.

Fifth, he took on the might of some 'satraps' of the Tata group—capable leaders who had grown up under J.R.D. Tata but who were running their respective companies largely as their own fiefdoms—and thus aligned all Tata companies to the strategic directions highlighted above.

By undertaking these essential and fundamental actions within his first few years as chairman, Ratan Tata ensured that the Tata group did not disintegrate and it also became future-ready. This was perhaps a more comprehensive transformation than anything the group had witnessed over the past century.

2000s: Second Decade as Chairman

By the early 2000s, Ratan Tata had grown in confidence and stature, and had also completed much of the fundamental restructuring of the group that was essential to its future. This enabled him to launch a series of bold strategic moves which would come to define his second decade as the chairman.

Foremost amongst these moves was his drive to globalize the group, not merely through a worldwide presence but also by inducing amongst Tata companies a global mindset and an urge to achieve world-class excellence. However, it was the big-ticket acquisitions that made the headlines. These included Tetley Tea, Corus, Jaguar Land Rover, Brunner Mond and Daewoo. They catapulted the Tata group onto the global stage almost immediately.

In addition to this, in 2004, Tata Sons also completed the initial public offering (IPO) of a Tata company which had already gone global: Tata Consultancy Services (TCS). This immensely successful IPO would result in the creation of the most valuable company (by market capitalization) of the Tata group. TCS would soon become a bellwether of sorts for the Indian corporate world.

Then, in 2008, Ratan Tata launched one of the greatest innovations undertaken by any Indian company: the Tata Nano, a small car for India. While the car itself was not a commercial success, it set new benchmarks in the automobile industry.

In 2008, the Government of India awarded Ratan Tata the Padma Vibhushan, the country's second-highest civilian honour, recognizing the breadth and depth of his contributions to Indian industry.

2010s: Retirement and Succession

In December 2012, Ratan Tata retired from his role as chairman of Tata Sons after twenty-one years in this leadership role and fifty years of working with the Tata group. It had been an extraordinary tenure by any standards, marked by both the transformation of the Tata institution into a coherent group as well as its rapid growth. Cyrus Mistry was selected as his successor in Tata Sons.

Ratan Tata was conferred the title of chairman emeritus of the company, and he also continued to helm the Tata Trusts as chairman. At the Tata Trusts, he led many impactful social initiatives, foremost amongst which was the fight against cancer, with investment in several hospitals and cancer care centres across the country.

However, Ratan Tata's retirement did not proceed as expected. Less than four years after Ratan had stepped down, on 24 October 2016, Tata Sons announced that its board of directors had replaced Cyrus Mistry as chairman of Tata Sons. The board also named Ratan Tata as interim chairman of Tata Sons, and constituted a selection committee to choose a new chairman. Consequently, at the age of seventy-nine, Ratan Tata stepped in once again as interim chairman for around four months, until a new chairman was appointed in February 2017.

In the meanwhile, an intense battle had begun, with Cyrus Mistry reacting strongly to his replacement by the board of Tata Sons. A long-drawn legal fight also followed, with two companies from the SP Group, which are shareholders of Tata Sons and are owned and controlled by the Mistry family, filing a petition against Tata Sons and others, alleging mismanagement and oppression of minority shareholders. The context and details of this fight have been narrated in other publications. This matter was finally decided by the Supreme Court of India, which ruled in favour of the Tata group.

2020s: The Final Years

After handing over the chairmanship of Tata Sons for a second time—this time to N. Chandrasekaran (Chandra), a Tata veteran who had led the phenomenal growth of TCS—Ratan Tata appeared happy and comfortable.

In his final few years, he was the elder statesman and mentor to Indian industry, both to the Tata group and to a number of young start-ups in which he had personally invested both time and money.

In 2020, along with Chandra, he spearheaded the Tata group's immediate and broad-based response to COVID-19, pledging a significant amount of Rs 1500 crore to fight against the pandemic. This amount was invested in urgently needed measures such as creating new hospital beds, providing personal protective equipment to frontline workers and meals to migrant workers, funding emergency medical treatment and conducting vaccination camps.

In April 2022, in one of his last major appearances on a public dais, Ratan Tata travelled to Assam for the launch of seven state-of-the-art cancer care hospitals, which were a joint initiative of Tata Trusts and the Government of Assam. Standing alongside the Prime Minister of India, Ratan Tata said, 'I dedicate my last years to health.'

Ratan Tata's own health, however, continued to trouble him. While he remained active until the final weekend before he passed away, it was clear to observers that he was finding it difficult to walk comfortably. In early October 2024, he was admitted to the Breach Candy Hospital in Mumbai. Close to midnight on 9 October, he breathed his last in the city where he had been born eighty-six years ago.

His passing was not merely the end of his life on Earth, it was the end of an era for Indian industry. He had served India and the Tatas with distinction and dedication for over sixty years and had transformed the Tata group. He had been a strong, unflinching torchbearer of Tata values.

But it would be unfair to associate him only with the Tata group, because he belonged to the nation at large. For many years now, he had been a role model and icon, admired, adored and loved by millions of Indians. The entire country mourned him, and every part of India celebrated his life.

A Multifaceted Life

As this brief summary has highlighted, Ratan Tata had many different facets.

He was a pioneer who took the Tata group into new and uncharted areas, such as passenger cars, and onto the global stage.

He was an outstanding industrialist who steered the rapid and profitable growth of the Tata group.

He was a technologist whose love for technology and insight into new technologies injected a new mindset into the Tatas.

He was an architect with an instinctive eye for aesthetics and design.

He was a transformative leader who brought a fractious and loose set of Tata companies together into a tightly woven group with a singular and strong identity.

He was a philanthropist who led the country's fight against cancer through Tata Trusts and contributed significantly to many other urgent social causes across the country.

He was a big supporter of young start-ups in India, going out of his way to personally invest in and provide both inspiration and support to some of the most innovative and daring start-ups that came up during the final two decades of his life.

Doing the Right Thing

Each of these facets are inspiring and deserves its own story. However, in this book, rather than addressing any of these life slices individually, I have chosen to speak to a single theme that cuts through all of them. This theme is Ratan Tata's constant urge, resolve and capability to do what is right.

I believe that this urge drove Ratan Tata's thoughts and actions in everything he did, whether it was in his role as pioneer, industrialist, leader or philanthropist. I have reached this conclusion based on conversations with many people who have worked closely with him, on my readings about him, and on my observations drawn from nearly four decades of working with the Tata group. Equally importantly, my belief is also based on what Ratan Tata has himself said on this subject.

He was asked about his legacy by the in-house magazine of the Tata group, *Tata Review*, in December 2012. Here is what he said:

> I have been asked that question before and I have always dodged it. That's because it is for others to decide [what my legacy is], not for me. The legacy I leave behind—that

> which I am aware of, that which I can express—is that I myself have lived by the principles that I have desired for the group. I have led by example in that sense, and I have devoted my life, as best as I could, to the welfare of the group. I have endeavoured to do the best I could with the responsibilities I have had. I have always tried to do the right thing.

See how he concludes this answer—'I have always tried to do the right thing.' In his own mind, this short sentence appears to summarize his approach towards work and life.

Two people who knew Ratan Tata well are his half-sisters, Deanna J. Jejeebhoy and Shireen J. Jejeebhoy. In a piece they wrote at the time of his retirement in 2012, they also touched on this very same aspect. They said of their half-brother: 'He takes great pride in doing the right thing, and this extends into his personal life as well.'

But what exactly does 'doing the right thing' mean? Is this just a broad catch-all phrase which sounds nice and good but means little or nothing in precise terms, a platitude of sorts? Or is it a specific, useful and inspiring philosophy of life which we can all learn from? In the next chapter, we see what this really meant to Ratan Tata, and how it shaped his life.

2

Doing the Right Thing: What Does It Really Mean?

To understand Ratan Tata's obsession with always 'doing the right thing', we should step back into history by around a century, to the times of his great-grandfather, Jamsetji Tata. Jamsetji founded the Tata group in 1868 and is widely acknowledged as the father of modern Indian industry. He passed away in 1904, thirty-three years before the birth of Ratan. Therefore, Ratan did not have the opportunity to meet him, but he was clearly inspired by Jamsetji's principles.

Humata, Hukhta, Huvarshta

Jamsetji Tata came from a family of Parsi priests, and he was deeply influenced by the Zoroastrian religion. In fact, when he chose a crest for his family, it bore the three

Avestan words 'Humata, Hukhta, Huvarshta', which mean 'Good thoughts, good words, good deeds'. Perhaps there cannot be a more succinct articulation for what doing the right thing means.

These three words encapsulate the ethical principles of the Zoroastrian religion. At first glance, they appear broadly similar to the wonderful Buddhist proverb 'See no evil, hear no evil, speak no evil'. But on closer examination, we see that the three Hs of Zoroastrianism are far more active in their intent than the Buddhist phrase, because they are all about what one should do, rather than what one should not do.

'Humata, Hukhta, Huvarshta' does not imply that we should engage in discrete thoughts or acts of goodness from time to time. On the other hand, they are about a permanent state of mind that focuses on being good at every moment in our lives. When Jamsetji Tata put these words on his family crest, he was also articulating, perhaps for the first time, the values which the Tata group should embody.

For many years, this crest was displayed on a wall in the foyer of Bombay House, the headquarters of the Tata group located in Mumbai. Ratan would have seen this crest each time he passed through the entrance of this stately building, and he would have come across these three words many times at other places too, whenever he reflected on Jamsetji and the heritage of the group.

It is quite likely that Ratan saw in these three words the essence of what the Tatas stood for, and he adopted these values as his own. It is also likely that these Zoroastrian values which appeared on the Tata crest were emphasized to him during his childhood by his grandmother, Lady Navajbai Tata, under whose care he spent considerable time. She was the wife of Jamsetji Tata's younger son, and had seen and interacted with Jamsetji himself. She had a deep impact on young Ratan's thinking. In the course of time, 'doing the right thing' became, I think, his own simple but powerful interpretation of 'Humata, Hukhta, Huvarshta'.

How did Ratan Tata put this philosophy into action in his own life and career? To the best of my knowledge, he has not dwelt on this subject himself. However, an examination of his long career with the Tata group, which lasted over sixty years, throws up some clear patterns and themes of what 'doing the right thing' meant to him.

I have been able to identify eight such themes. They are summarized below, and each of these facets will be covered in detail in the subsequent chapters of this book.

1. Custodian of the Tata Legacy

For Ratan Tata, one of the most important facets of doing the right thing was protecting and nurturing the Tata legacy. In his role as chairman of the Tata group, he considered himself as the custodian of this legacy, which had begun with the values and principles established by Jamsetji Tata more than a century earlier.

Sidharth Sharma, general counsel of Tata Sons and a good friend, recollected an interaction with Ratan Tata where Sidharth mentioned to him, in a particular context, the need to safeguard Ratan's own legacy. Ratan turned to him and said, softly but firmly, that it was not 'his' legacy. On the other hand, he was the custodian of the Tata legacy, and that was most important.

For the head of any institution, keeping intact the organization's values and legacy is one of his or her most important fiduciary responsibilities. This is true of all well-meaning and established businesses. In the case of the Tata group, it is perhaps not just important but mission-critical, because it is an institution which has stood by its values of integrity, excellence, pioneering and giving back to the community for over 150 years, without being swayed by the winds of time. It is this steadfastness which has powered the success of Tata across six generations and made the house of Tata so different from many other business houses in the country. This would undoubtedly have weighed on Ratan's mind, because as chairman, he was now responsible for carrying forward this baton.

As you will read in a later chapter of this book, many bold decisions that Ratan took, and many new paths that he embarked on, were clearly driven by this overarching objective. In fact, as I will argue, if the Tata group has stayed as a single coherent group post the days of J.R.D. Tata, it is because of the firm directions charted by Ratan Tata. I think some of these decisions also took a toll on him. Yet he persisted, demonstrating how important it was for him to serve as a true custodian of the institution whose leadership had been entrusted to him.

2. Putting the Nation First

To Ratan, the nation always came first. He was driven by his dreams for his country, and doing the right thing for India was, I think, his foremost goal. He was seized by the fact that the Tatas have always been driven by the spirit of nation-building, ever since the days of Jamsetji Tata.

Narendra Modi, prime minister of India, authored an article paying tribute to Ratan Tata around a month after Ratan had passed away. It is rare to see such an article written by a prime minister about an industrialist. The prime minister ends this beautiful piece by saying, 'Generations will be grateful to him [Ratan Tata] for making India a better, kinder and more hopeful place.'

N. Chandrasekaran, chairman of Tata Sons, wrote a lovely, spontaneous piece on the social media platform LinkedIn, paying tribute to Ratan Tata soon after his demise. In this tribute, he says, 'Anybody who met Mr Tata came away with a story about his humanity, warmth and his dreams for India. There really was no one like him.'

Both these statements attest to Ratan Tata's constant urge to do his best for India. Virtually every person whom I have interviewed while doing the research for this book has spoken about the primacy of India in Ratan's thought processes. Many have specifically mentioned that the country always came first for Ratan. They have added that, where required, he would prioritize the needs of the nation above the business requirements of the Tata group.

3. Ethical Conduct of Business

Principled conduct of business was a lodestar of Ratan's life. Every single episode that I have heard or read about tells me that acting ethically in business was, to him, non-negotiable. Doing the right thing clearly meant acting in a manner which was honest and upright, without any hesitation, and notwithstanding any impact on the business.

This is a topic that Ratan has spoken and written about on more than one occasion, so his own thoughts on the subject are quite clearly there for all of us to see. Take, for instance, the epilogue that he wrote to the book *The Creation of Wealth*, authored by R.M. Lala. Here, Ratan talks about what kind of business enterprise he would like the Tatas to be: 'the predominant business house in India, which amidst fast eroding values, will continue to stand out as being a well-integrated, growth-oriented group with market leadership, operating with a high level of integrity, a great value system and uncompromising in its goal to achieve results without partaking in corruption, bribery or political influence.'

This is a particularly courageous stance to take in a country such as India, where corrupt practices and political nexus have been known to often deliver quick results. And yet, this stance defined the Ratan Tata approach to business. For him, 'doing the right thing' meant always making ethical choices, even if this implied letting economically valuable business opportunities pass by. You will read some inspiring stories later in this book which bring this facet alive.

4. Beyond Legal Compliance: Being Morally Correct

For Ratan Tata, doing the right thing went beyond mere legal compliance. Being totally compliant with the law was essential, but what was far more important to him was being morally correct even if this meant going well beyond legal compliance.

Ishaat Hussain, who served as executive director and chief financial officer (CFO) at Tata Sons, worked closely with Ratan Tata for several years. Ishaat is also a keen observer of people, and his observations about Ratan struck me as very insightful. Speaking to me, he emphasized how moral courage and being correct from all relevant perspectives was fundamental to the way Ratan Tata conducted the affairs of the Tata group. 'He often told us that we must not only be seen to be doing the right thing as per law, but we must be doing what we believe is truly correct.'

In my analysis, this impulse came to Ratan Tata from three different sources. First, the Tata group and its leaders had always done what they thought was correct, even if it was not required by law. Ratan would have been familiar with many of these legends and stories, dating back to the days of earlier Tata chairmen such as Jamsetji Tata and Dorabji Tata. Second, his mentor and predecessor as chairman, J.R.D. Tata, took great pride in being morally correct in all his actions. Ratan would have observed him at close quarters. Third, this moral compass appears to have been an integral part of Ratan's upbringing and was deeply embedded in his mindset. Perhaps his grandmother, Lady Navajbai Tata, played a key role in making this happen. In addition, maybe this impulse was just intrinsic to the kind of person he was.

5. Fostering Fairness

The importance of being totally fair to all stakeholders in any call that he took was a critical element of Ratan Tata's decision-making process. Some people who have worked with him have mentioned to me that he often agonized over this aspect and also engaged in long discussions with his close colleagues before reaching a settled position on what was the fair way forward in any situation.

Talking about how he arrives at decisions, Ratan Tata once said in an interview with an internal Tata group publication in 2006: 'As you think the decision through, you have to automatically feel that this is wrong, incorrect or unfair. You have to think of the advantages and disadvantages to the segments involved, be it employees or (other) stakeholders.'

Ratan Tata was perhaps acutely aware that many of the decisions he took as chairman of the Tata group would have a wide-ranging and long-term impact. In addition, many of the issues that he needed to address in his corner office were complex matters involving multiple stakeholders, both internal and external. It is likely that both these factors heightened in his mind the importance of fairness as a critical element of doing the right thing.

6. Care and Compassion

Genuine care and compassion for people was at the heart of Ratan Tata's leadership philosophy. He felt a deep sense of responsibility towards Tata employees, as well as for other stakeholders of the group. Of all aspects that went into doing the right thing, perhaps this was first and foremost in his mind.

I experienced this first-hand when I ran into a personal issue during the mid-2000s. I requested an appointment with Ratan Tata to explain the matter and for some specific help. He provided me a meeting immediately. I recall speaking with him in his suite at the Taj West End Hotel in Bengaluru, during one of his visits to the city. He heard me out patiently and said that he would do his best to help. Within fifteen days of this meeting, he provided me with a resolution. I found this amazing, particularly given that he kept to such a hectic schedule and had so many important official matters on his plate.

I have heard similar stories from many of my Tata colleagues. Amidst his never-ending work commitments, Ratan would inevitably prioritize the needs of his people, demonstrating his care for them. Over the course of his career, he developed an instinctive understanding of the issues that people working closely with him were facing at any point in time, and he would then support them, often in his own silent way, in addressing these matters.

In addition, his care and compassion for dogs was legendary. He was always there for his pet dogs, and would prioritize their health and wellness over many other activities. Such care was not limited to his own pets. He would go out of his way to find homes for other dogs too. Some of these heart-warming stories are narrated later in this book.

7. Respect for People

Ratan Tata treated people with grace and respect, notwithstanding their seniority or level. This was integral to his personality. For him, doing the right thing meant being gentlemanly in all his interactions.

Two senior directors who have worked with Ratan closely, Ishaat Hussain and R.K. Krishna Kumar, have both told me that one of Ratan's strongest beliefs was that one should never ever impinge on a person's dignity. A direct outcome of this belief was Ratan's courteous behaviour as well as his humble demeanour.

During meetings, he would listen carefully, even to the junior-most manager in the room. I have once seen him at a lunch table at the Tata Management Training Centre, Pune, listening silently and with focused attention to six junior officers seated around him. Later, he took care to shake hands courteously with all of them before he left the table. His office or he would respond meticulously and courteously to thousands of letters and emails that he received. All these were expressions of respect.

I am told that when he was upset, he would demonstrate his unhappiness quite clearly through his body language. But he would never raise his voice, or use intemperate or rough language, perhaps because he thought this would be hurtful to the person he was interacting with. Such restraint is quite rare amongst leaders in today's business world. On the other hand, many people in positions of power are known to treat their underlings with arrogance, even as they pander to their superiors.

8. Meeting Every Commitment

One of my all-time favourite Ratan Tata quotes is the phrase 'A promise is a promise'. This is such a powerful, memorable and pithy phrase, and I use it whenever I speak about lessons that we can learn from Ratan Tata. He uttered these words during the launch event of the Tata Nano. However, this sentiment extended to every part of his life. For him, meeting every commitment that he made, however large or small, was a way of life, and it was the right thing to do.

From the interviews I conducted while researching for this book, it became quite clear to me that once Ratan made a commitment to anyone, his mind would not rest until he had delivered on his promise. This was not necessarily on major corporate issues of importance, it could be as simple or minor a matter as a commitment just to meet someone. If Ratan told you that he would meet you, you could be sure that he would make this happen, regardless of all the other pressures on his time.

Meeting every commitment is perhaps the best way of establishing trust. In Ratan Tata's case, I think his urge to redeem every promise he made went much deeper than the desire to be seen as trustworthy. This was the way he was built, and it was part of his being. He always held himself to his words.

Eight Themes of 'Doing the Right Thing'

We have now covered eight themes of what 'doing the right thing' meant to Ratan Tata. I think that each of these themes steered and influenced his behaviour. One or more of these individual themes would take prominence at various points, depending on the specific issue at hand. In aggregate, they represented a sort of personal guidebook which was always in his mind as he grappled with decisions of various shapes and sizes. Many of these decisions involved complex issues with no simple or straightforward solutions.

These eight themes moved 'doing the right thing' from an abstract philosophy to a well-defined framework of decision-making that took centre stage in Ratan's life and career.

In the chapters that follow, I will illustrate these themes and their nuances through real-life stories drawn from Ratan Tata's life. I will also explore each theme in greater detail, drawing from these rich experiences.

I would like to highlight an important point here, before we move forward. In this book, I have considered each of these themes from Ratan Tata's perspective—in other words, I address Ratan's pursuit of what he thought was the right thing to do, under each of these eight themes. His deep conviction that following a certain path was the right course of action led Ratan to walking that path, and that is what he constantly endeavoured to do.

However, one man's firm conviction that a certain course of action is the right thing to do may not find uniform acceptance with everyone else. A second person may feel that some other course of action is the right path to pursue, and a third person may feel that there is yet another course of action which is the correct one. These choices depend on many factors, including what values and beliefs each of us hold in the highest priority.

Hence, this book is specifically about what Ratan Tata believed was the right thing to do in various circumstances, and there may be cases where you do not necessarily agree with the specific choices he made. In my view, that is perfectly fine, provided you are being true to the values which mean the most to you. It would be useful to bear this perspective in mind, as you progress to reading these stories in the chapters ahead.

Before I end this chapter, I would also like to point out that these stories are interesting episodes from Ratan's long career with the Tata group. At one level, therefore, they can be read and enjoyed as nice tales from the life of an iconic individual. I do hope that you will relish them for this reason.

But at another level, they are also stories with meaning which hold invaluable learnings for us, because 'doing the right thing' is as relevant to our own lives as it was to

Ratan's life. Whether we are chairpersons, directors, entrepreneurs, professionals working in corporates, homemakers or students, we desire to lead good, meaningful lives where we can grow, achieve our goals and contribute our best. This requires us to do the right thing ourselves, and this is where these stories shine an invaluable light for us, because they illustrate why and how Ratan did what he thought was right. Viewed in this context, this book can serve both as an inspiration and a practical guide.

This is why I have chosen to write this book. This is also why I will urge you to turn the page and read on.

3

Custodian of the Tata Legacy

On 25 March 1991, Ratan Tata was appointed chairman of the Tata group. He succeeded J.R.D. Tata, who had been in this role for a remarkably long period of fifty-three years. In assuming this position, Ratan also became the de facto chief custodian of the Tata legacy. This was a rich legacy that dated back to 1868, when Jamsetji Tata founded the Tata group. It was a legacy that had thereafter been kept more or less intact over several decades by Ratan's predecessors as chairman: J.R.D. Tata, Nowroji Saklatvala and Dorabji Tata. Ratan was now the fifth incumbent in this chair, and suddenly, the future of Tata was his to evolve, nurture and shape.

What did 'doing the right thing' mean to him in this context? Here are three stories that highlight what this meant: building a cohesive Tata group, making Tata future-ready, and finally, leading transformation at Tata Trusts.

Building a Cohesive Tata Group

As custodian of Tata, the first task that Ratan set himself was ensuring the long-term survival and sustenance of the group. Tata had grown and flourished for over 120 years, and yet, in Ratan's mind, the future of the group was at serious risk. In fact, exactly ten years before he became chairman, Ratan had expressed his anxieties in a letter to J.R.D. Tata. Here is what he said in his letter dated 29 July 1981 (which was also J.R.D.'s seventy-seventh birthday):

> There is a growing feeling amongst some of us that the Tatas are no longer operating as a unified organization, but instead as diverse fragments under a common name. There is therefore in my view an urgent need to arrest and reverse this trend ... I honestly believe we are losing the strength and synergy inherent in a group of our size and diversity.

Why did Ratan Tata feel like this, particularly when the external world had a far more positive view about the Tata group? For instance, the day after Ratan Tata assumed charge as chairman, India's largest business newspaper, the *Economic Times*, had written, on 26 March 1991:

> Under Mr (J.R.D.) Tata's leadership, the group has earned a special place in India's corporate life in two important ways. First, it has professionalized management to a degree that few other indigenous business houses have done, and done it to a point where professionals have emerged as corporate stars in their own right. Second, it has consistently stayed in tune with national priorities, and ventured into the fields which urgently required private investment.

Did Ratan not agree with this assessment of the group?

The reasons that Ratan felt anxious about the future of the group were largely internal. He knew that from an external perspective, Tata enjoyed a spotless reputation for integrity and nation-building, both of which had been carefully nurtured by his predecessor, J.R.D. Tata. In fact, J.R.D. Tata was his mentor, the man who had shaped his thinking. Ratan Tata has spoken about J.R.D.'s integrity and his social consciousness, his thoughtfulness and care, all of which had gone into building a great Tata edifice during J.R.D.'s long tenure as chairman.

On the other hand, it is likely that the following points were causing Ratan great concern.

First, the Tata group was not working as a cohesive institution. On the other hand, it had become quite disjointed in its functioning. J.R.D. Tata had held the group together through the sheer force of his iconic personality and his powers of persuasion. He was universally respected as an inspiring leader and a father figure, and therefore, in specific matters where he intervened, companies largely went by what he said. However, many individual Tata companies, steered by established and formidable leaders, were busy crafting their own futures, and were not willing to accede to central direction or control from the headquarters of the group, particularly in matters of strategy or people.

Perhaps such lack of central control was also the result of government policies, in particular the Monopolies and Restrictive Trade Practices (MRTP) Act, 1969. If the group had been run as a tight, cohesive and unified whole, it may well have fallen foul of some provisions of this Act, and, as a result, would not have been permitted licences to expand or venture into new areas of business. However, by the time Ratan Tata became chairman, economic liberalization had been set in motion in India by Prime Minister P.V. Narasimha Rao and Finance Minister Manmohan Singh. This had brought about big changes, and licensing had, in fact, been eliminated in many sectors of the economy.

Second, the parent company of the Tatas, Tata Sons, held surprisingly low equity stakes in many major companies of the group. For example, in 1991, Tata Sons had only single-digit equity stakes in Tata Steel, Tata Motors and Tata Power. In fact, at one point in time, the Birla group had a far higher stake in Tata Steel than Tata Sons. All this made such companies vulnerable to hostile takeovers by other Indian or global groups—and this was now a real possibility post the onset of economic reforms. In addition, did Tata Sons have a real and formal right to manage companies in which it held such minuscule ownership? Ratan Tata had mentioned that this was one of the first issues that struck him when he became chairman.

Third, while companies of the group used a common name, Tata, there was no unified look and feel for this brand, nor were there any guidelines pertaining to its use.

This had resulted in different companies using widely differing versions of the Tata logo. Just as an example, Tata Motors (then called TELCO) used a 'T' which looked totally grey, rigid and metallic, whereas Tata Tea (the company where I began my career in Tata) used a very different flexible version of a 'T' crafted from two green tea leaves! In addition, there was no common understanding of what the brand stood for. If such drift had continued, the Tata brand would have got increasingly fragmented, muddled and lost over the next several years.

It is against this background that Ratan Tata donned the mantle of custodian of the Tata legacy. For him, 'doing the right thing' meant taking the actions that would ensure the continued unity and survival of the Tatas, while simultaneously ensuring that the group remained steadfastly committed to its values. It also meant developing and executing these plans with urgency, however difficult they may be. There was no time to lose.

So what did Ratan Tata do? He knew that for a group as large as the Tatas, and with even greater growth ambitions for the future, strong ownership, institutional processes and robust frameworks would be needed to hold it together—a towering personality alone would not suffice. And he set about taking some key actions which would define the future structure and some fundamental governing processes of the group.

To begin with, Ratan Tata focused his attention on raising the low equity stakes that Tata Sons held in many Tata companies. This would give the Tata group a 'legal right' to manage these companies. Equally importantly, this would also ensure that these companies would be shielded from hostile takeovers. Ratan's target was to raise the Tata Group's equity shareholding in all major Tata companies to at least 26 per cent from the then existing single-digit levels.

Achieving this target required Tata Sons to put out significant funding to purchase large additional chunks of equity shares. To enable this in an astute manner, Ratan relied on the wise counsel of Noshir Soonawala, who served as his CFO and also became his close confidant over several years. For some of the funding, they were able to utilize the positive cash flows generated by TCS, which was then a division of Tata Sons. In addition, in 1995, just four years after Ratan had become chairman, Tata Sons embarked on a major rights issue of its own ordinary shares.

The manner in which this rights issue was implemented—why and how Tata Trusts, the majority shareholders of Tata Sons, renounced their rights, and how some major Tata companies then bought these renounced shares to ensure that ownership remained within the Tata group—is a case study in itself. Without getting into details here, suffice it to say that the funds raised through this rights issue were then utilized to increase equity stakes in key companies of the group. This gave Tata Sons a right to manage these companies. Without this major effort to raise equity stakes, it is quite likely that large companies of the Tata group, such as Tata Steel, Tata Power and Tata Motors, could have slipped out of Tata control during the subsequent years. This may appear inconceivable today, when each of these companies is seen as such an integral part of the Tata empire, but it is the truth.

Ratan Tata's second big move to establish a cohesive Tata group was a clear and concerted initiative to establish a unified identity for the Tata brand. Until then, companies had been using various 'Tata' logos of their own making—there was no uniformity, and there was no agreement either in place for how exactly the brand should be used. Ratan engaged the services of Wolff Olins, a reputed British design agency, to develop a new corporate group mark and logo for the Tata brand. He wanted a modern, world-class logo that would stand the test of time. It took over one and a half years of intense work and discussion to evolve the new Tata logo and brand identity plan. This simple, powerful and well-crafted logo continues to proudly represent the Tata brand until today.

Then, by 1998, he put in place a comprehensive agreement called the Brand Equity and Business Promotion (BEBP) agreement which provided companies of the group the right to use the unified Tata brand for a small licence fee, and also prescribed clear guidelines for its usage. Companies could choose not to sign this agreement, but then they would not have the right to use the Tata name. Very importantly, this BEBP agreement listed the requirements a company had to meet if it wished to use the Tata name and brand.

For instance, each company signing this agreement would have to adhere to the Tata Code of Conduct, which laid down the ethical principles that would govern all aspects of business. In addition, each company would have to become part of a business excellence framework defined by the group. This was the very first time in the history of the Tata group that the relationship between the group and its companies was being formalized in this manner.

Between these two big initiatives—the shoring up of Tata Sons' equity stakes in group companies and the BEBP agreement—Ratan Tata laid the foundations of a cohesive Tata group within the first decade of his tenure as chairman. With the first initiative, Tata Sons reinforced its right to manage its companies and also protected them from possible hostile takeovers. With the second, Tata Sons ensured that the companies knew exactly what obligations they had to discharge and what standards of excellence they had to meet for the privilege of using the Tata name.

There was one more step that Ratan took to ensure a cohesive group. Through the introduction of a well-structured retirement policy, he ensured that powerful satraps such as Russi Mody, who were running individual Tata companies somewhat like their own empires, gave way to leaders who were far more aligned to a Tata group where unity mattered as much as diversity.

Doing the right thing through such comprehensive restructuring of an established organization is inevitably fraught with resistance to change. In this case too, the going was not always easy. Ratan's battles with satraps like

Russi Mody and Ajit Kerkar have been well-documented in many other publications, and so in the interest of brevity, I will choose not to repeat these stories here. Similarly, the BEBP agreement also ran into opposition in some quarters and had its share of critics as well before it was eventually approved by the boards of all major Tata companies.

Pause for a moment and consider the immensity of what Ratan Tata had achieved here through these major acts of restructuring. These were not just big moves, they were fundamental to the continued existence of a strong, unified and coherent Tata group. Personally, I feel that the Tata group as we know it today would not exist had these bold actions not been taken by Ratan way back in the 1990s.

Making Tata Future-Ready

In 1997, I was a young marketing and sales manager at Tata Tea. One morning, my colleagues and I were called in for a session to talk about a new framework: the Tata Business Excellence Model (TBEM). I recall that session vividly. It focused on how each of us should work towards ensuring the consistent quality of processes within our business, whether they be customer-facing processes or internal processes such as strategy formulation or people development. We were introduced to seven different categories under which our business processes and results would be assessed. We were also informed that our business would be assessed and scored by an independent team every year under all these heads.

This was the first time I had heard of TBEM, which would soon become a strong backbone of excellence within the Tata group. The clear objective of this framework was that each Tata company should gear up to deliver market-leading performance on a sustained basis, for which robust processes in every area of business were essential.

Within a couple of years thereafter, I was invited to a Tata group meeting called the Annual Group Management Meeting. We were, I recall, around 400 of us in the conference hall. On the dais were Ratan Tata and members of the Group Corporate Centre of Tata Sons, all of them senior directors.

Ratan Tata then stood up to address us. His primary focus was the need for us to pull up our socks and ensure excellent business performance. He laid out three clear objectives: every business had to be within the top three in its industry in terms of market share and profits, had to deliver positive EVA (economic value added), and had to build size and scale commensurate with its sector. We were asked to prepare business plans with these three objectives in mind and bring them for review to a Business Review Committee (BRC) which had been constituted for this purpose.

Immediately thereafter, this planning exercise began in right earnest. I recall being part of the team at Tata Tea which was tasked by our then CEO to work on our company's five-year business plan. To the best of my knowledge, this was the first such formal long-term planning exercise in the company with clear objectives laid down, and it was an intensive effort which lasted several weeks. Many new perspectives and fresh ideas emerged during these discussions, including new horizons for profitable growth and new investments that would be required to make this happen. At the Tata group, the push for performance and for becoming future-ready had begun in right earnest.

To understand the background in which all this happened, we should rewind a few years to 25 March 1991, when Ratan Tata was appointed chairman of Tata Sons. Just four months later, on 24 July 1991, Manmohan Singh, who had been appointed finance minister of India, presented his maiden budget where he quoted Victor Hugo's famous words: 'No power on earth can stop an idea whose time has come.' This landmark budget, perhaps the most important in the history of independent India, put forward a framework for liberalization, privatization and globalization—in effect, opening up the Indian economy to the world at large. It also removed several restrictions on Indian companies and, very importantly, eliminated the need for licensing in most sectors of the economy, thus creating, in one stroke, multiple opportunities for growth.

Ratan Tata quickly grasped the significance of this budget and its possible impact on the Tata group. He knew that foreign firms would soon enter India since the economy was now far more open. The Tata companies had to be strong enough to withstand this new era of global competition. He also knew that if the Tata companies had to leverage the new liberalized economy, they needed to be ready for a very different future. In this context, he saw that there was only one path to doing the right thing for the group that he was leading: He had to make Tata future-ready. It was a tough path, which required a lot of soul-searching and remedial action.

He engaged the services of the global consulting firm McKinsey to assess the state of readiness of the Tata companies and also to suggest what the group should do to grow rapidly in the new liberalized economy. McKinsey submitted a candid report which recommended significant restructuring of the group, with a focus on a few core sectors. The report also said that many Tata companies were totally unprepared to cope with the future and were in substantial danger of falling behind their competitors. This was the reality that Ratan Tata now had to address.

Tata Business Excellence Model

One clear way forward was to ensure that the Tata companies developed a mindset of excellence, while benchmarking themselves against the best in their respective industries. This was the genesis of the Tata Business Excellence Model, which I have referred to earlier in this section. TBEM was launched in 1998, building on the JRD-QV award which had been announced four years earlier, with a stated ambition of driving significant business improvements in the Tata group.

Under the JRD-QV award and thereafter under TBEM, every company would be assessed by an independent team and rated on a maximum score of 1000 points. This overall score would emerge from scores for seven categories: leadership, strategy, customer and market focus, information and analysis, people focus, process management and business results. A company that scored above 600 points would be eligible for the JRD-QV award, which soon became the top internal recognition within the Tata group.

Even more importantly, TBEM assessments were designed to throw up both strengths and opportunities for improvement (commonly referred to as OFIs within the group). Companies had to work on their OFIs, and ensure steady improvement on these before the next assessment cycle came on. I recall that, as a manager at Tanishq and then at the Titan watches business, I had a clear list of OFIs identified by each TBEM assessment, which my team and I would then have to address and achieve tangible progress on. This was equally true of thousands of my colleagues across Tata companies. Overall, this quickly led to a virtuous cycle of improvement in every area of the business.

With the launch of TBEM, Ratan Tata had put in place a quest for the holy grail of excellence that spread like wildfire across the group. Over the course of the next decade, most Tata businesses made great strides in establishing strong business processes, which in turn began producing positive financial and operational results.

Many years later, in 2008, Ratan Tata wrote the first chapter of a book titled *Business of Excellence*, where he reflected on the initial days of TBEM. Here are some excerpts from this chapter which provide an insight into his thinking:

> That was a time when many of our Companies had their heads in the sand. The dominant impression was that we were less nimble than others, more resistant to change and extremely set in our ways. What we needed to do was to benchmark ourselves with the brightest and the best, and get away from doing things the way we had done them in the past. The Tata Business Excellence Model set the tone and created the foundation for what, I believe, was one of the more critical transformation initiatives that the group had undertaken in recent times.

He goes on to say:

> TBEM became the formal, explicit component of our drive for business excellence ... our quest for quality, for

excellence in business, should be never ending. This is not a voyage where you can rest your oars.

Business Review Committees

Ratan did not rest his oars, either. Alongside TBEM, he constituted Business Review Committees (BRC), to act as an important strategic bridge between Tata Sons and individual Tata companies. These committees were established under the umbrella of Tata Sons, with coordination by the Tata Strategic Management Group. They consisted of senior Tata directors nominated by the Group Corporate Centre. Each committee would focus on the business plans of one specific Tata company, reviewing and challenging these plans, putting forward new perspectives where relevant and also offering support and advice.

I remember attending two such BRC meetings as one of the chief operating officers (COO) at Titan. What I recall vividly are the wise observations of the senior directors who were members of the BRC as they sat through presentations on our future plans—sometimes pushing us to think further, and at other times striking notes of caution. A few clear actionable areas, primarily relating to growth levers, emerged at the end of these meetings.

Rajendra (Raju) Bhinge headed the Tata Strategic Management Group in those days, and worked closely with Ratan Tata for several years. He anchored this major effort under Ratan Tata's overall guidance, and recalls how major growth and investment plans were screened quite rigorously at the BRCs. He says that this system of pushing for profitable growth but with appropriate reviews, checks and balances worked very well.

By the mid-2000s, many Tata group companies were heading on the right trajectories towards meeting their objectives. Clearly, the BRCs had played their role in making this happen. Raju Bhinge goes on to say, quite evocatively, 'These BRCs were much like catalysts to get the right growth mindsets in place.'

Global Mindset

A third big drive that Ratan Tata personally championed to make the group future-ready—in addition to the TBEM and the BRCs—was a push towards globalization. The most visible element of this drive was the global marquee acquisitions undertaken by the Tatas under his leadership: the acquisitions of Tetley Tea, Corus Steel and Jaguar Land Rover. There were many others too, including Daewoo

Motors in South Korea, NatSteel in Singapore, Eight O'Clock Coffee in the USA, General Chemicals in the USA and Brunner Mond in the UK.

Many of these acquisitions have been written about extensively in other publications and books, so in the interests of brevity I will not cover the rationale, the chronological details or the critical evaluation of each acquisition here. If you wish to know more about the Tetley acquisition, which came in the year 2000 and was the forerunner amongst all these moves, you could refer to my earlier book *Tata Log* where I have narrated this story in great detail. If you would like to read more about the Corus or Jaguar Land Rover acquisitions, which were undertaken in 2007 and 2008 respectively, then I will refer you to the comprehensive biography of Ratan Tata (*Ratan Tata: A Life*), authored by Thomas Mathew. Suffice it to say that these were bold, even audacious moves for Tata, because until then, no Indian company had ever contemplated such large acquisitions of huge and reputed global brands and businesses.

Speaking to *Outlook*, the monthly magazine, of Andersen Consulting in January 2000, well before many of these acquisitions became reality, Ratan Tata articulated his thoughts on why globalization was important to the Tatas. He said, 'In general, as a group we have been very inward looking, seeing only India as our market. We have not focused adequately on growing overseas. Part of this was due to foreign exchange restrictions. Now that these restrictions have been eased extensively, we should be looking at growing overseas in a serious manner. By growing overseas, I don't mean just exporting our products but looking at acquisitions, alliances and things of this nature.'

One immediate result of these acquisitions was the metamorphosis of the Tata group from an inward-looking Indian organization to a confident, global enterprise of Indian origin. This confidence was not confined to the global markets alone, it had a positive impact on many Tata companies in India too, which now strode forward with a new spring in their step.

Let me illustrate this with my own feelings in 2000, when Tata Tea completed the Tetley acquisition. I was part of the marketing team in Tata Tea in those days, with the responsibility of managing some brands of tea in India. I could see around me that the Tetley acquisition gave our own Indian marketing and sales team a renewed sense of pride and a new confidence in competing with Unilever in the local markets. After all, if we had acquired the world's second largest tea brand, then the sky was the limit in India too.

Such confidence was important in a liberalized India, where many global companies had already made their entry. But Ratan's global push did not start or stop with these acquisitions alone. For him, globalization was also about Tata companies making world-class products and services, about benchmarking with the best in the world in everything the companies did. It was about leaders and managers of the group developing a 'global mindset' where they constantly measured themselves against the world's finest companies in their respective industries, shedding an India-insular vision. I recall Ratan Tata emphasizing this more than once in internal group meetings which I attended.

Such a global mindset was an important element in making Tata brands and businesses future-ready. Once again, I would like to illustrate this with an example from my own Tata career. Between 2005 and 2012, I served as the COO of the watches business in Titan Company, a Tata enterprise. Titan was already a strong market leader in India by then, and a consistently profitable business. But during this period, we began comparing our growth and financial metrics with the Swatch group of Switzerland, which we saw as a global benchmark. Bhaskar Bhat was the managing director of Titan at that time, and I reported to him. Even while we performed very well as a business in those years, his constant question to me would be, 'When can we reach and exceed the Swatch group, on our profit before taxes [PBT] as a percentage of revenues? When can we beat them on product innovation?'

Questions like these led us to undertake many internal exercises relating to areas such as design and innovation, manufacturing and sourcing processes and costs, marketing and retailing. We studied what the Swatch group and other global brands did in each of these areas and what we could learn from them. These initiatives went a long way towards making the Titan watches business even more competitive, robust and future-ready. Such questions were being asked not just in Titan, but across many Tata businesses—one of the key reasons for this was that Ratan Tata had pushed all of us to work with a global mindset.

These significant initiatives announced and championed by Ratan Tata—a sharp focus on performance, the TBEM, the BRCs and globalization—delivered a Tata group which was far more future-ready than ever before. Many companies of the group transformed themselves and seized market-leading positions in many industry sectors in the country, while ensuring that they stayed true to the Tata values of integrity and community focus.

For instance, Tata Steel, which was earlier bogged down by several inefficiencies that had accumulated over the years, revamped its cost structure, reinvented its customer focus and became a globally competitive firm. What is even more remarkable is that it did this while safeguarding the interests of its workers—including the workers who took separation from the company. Tata Power, on the other hand, undertook a different growth path to future-readiness—it achieved new scale by commissioning several new power projects during Ratan Tata's tenure as chairman, including expansion to new geographical areas.

In addition to these efforts in individual companies, the Tata group also entered many important new sectors during Ratan Tata's leadership—including retail, financial services, telecom and aerospace. Ratan Tata also led the divestment of businesses which, in his view, had no strategic importance to the future of the Tata group and would perhaps perform better in other hands. This included the sale of companies such as TOMCO (Tata Oil Mills Company) and Hitech Drilling.

Is there a yardstick by which we can measure the success of Ratan Tata's efforts to make the Tata group future-ready? Perhaps no single metric can capture this holistically. At a broad level, the continued growth and success of the group so many years after his tenure is testimony to how well he prepared Tata for the future. But a more immediate metric is the rapid growth that the group experienced during Ratan Tata's own tenure of twenty-one years at the helm of the Tata group.

In 1992, the first year after he assumed the role of chairman, the revenues of the group stood at Rs 14,092 crore ($5.8 billion, at that year's historical conversion rate). In 2012, the year in which he retired from his role as chairman of Tata Sons, revenues had grown dramatically to Rs 4,75,721 crore ($100 billion, again at that year's historical conversion rate). This was not just rapid growth, it was remarkable by any standards.

This was possible only because Ratan Tata did the right thing, in pushing relentlessly for performance, introducing new processes to drive excellence, making bold moves to expand the group's horizons, and thus ensuring that the group addressed both the opportunities and challenges of a liberalized economy.

Transformation at the Tata Trusts

At the core of the Tata group's legacy are the Tata Trusts. These trusts collectively own 66 per cent of the equity shares of Tata Sons, the holding company of the Tata group. They utilize the dividends which they obtain through this equity ownership to serve society through a range of philanthropic initiatives.

These trusts have, over the past several decades, established some of India's most iconic institutions, such as the Tata Memorial Hospital in Mumbai, the Tata Medical Centre in Kolkata, Tata Institute of Fundamental Research, Tata Institute of Social Sciences, National Centre for Performing Arts and a number of cancer care hospitals across the country. They have also contributed significantly over the years to a number of other important social needs such as disaster relief, education, healthcare, rural livelihoods, social justice, arts and culture.

In the famous words of J.R.D. Tata, the trusts ensure that 'what came from the people has gone back to the people many times over'.

Post his retirement as chairman of Tata Sons in 2012, Ratan Tata dedicated the final years of his life to renewing and strengthening the purpose and the fabric of the Tata Trusts. He considered this an integral part of his custodianship of the Tata legacy. This is the story of some key elements of the transformation that he drove during this period, as chairman of the Tata Trusts.

One of the significant moves that Ratan Tata led was bringing the operations of all the different Trusts together under the unified banner of 'Tata Trusts'. There are fourteen trusts housed under this banner, each of them a separate legal entity. The oldest of these is the JN Tata Endowment for the Higher Education of Indians, established in 1892 by the founder of the Tata group, Jamsetji Tata, himself. Then, there are the Sir Ratan Tata Trust and the Sir Dorabji Tata Trust, established in 1919 and 1932 respectively, by the two sons of the founder. There are eleven other trusts, each with mandates of their own.

Under Ratan Tata's leadership, a single powerful brand, 'Tata Trusts', was created as a virtual umbrella for all these charitable trusts. This resulted in greater and more focused external visibility, as well as a far more unified spirit within the entire organization. For the first time ever, all the trusts and most teams were housed physically in a single location—the World Trade Centre at Cuffe Parade in Mumbai. The operating structure, under a single managing trustee/chief executive officer and organization-wide functional heads, also reflected this approach. Some of my colleagues who have been employees of the trusts have told me how these moves broke through silos that may have existed earlier and created a unified team spirit.

I recall being invited by the Tata Trusts in 2017 to participate in discussions related to the 125th anniversary of the establishment of the trusts. I attended several meetings at the headquarters in World Trade Centre, and could see how integrated the operations of the trusts had become by then. I was also struck by the innovative approaches that the trusts were implementing, in their endeavour to address important social needs. This was quite different from the perception I had held previously, that the trusts were primarily givers of charitable grants.

This approach was, once again, led by Ratan Tata's transformative thinking, which redefined the trusts' mission and moved them from traditional charity to focused, proactive, result-oriented and systemic philanthropy. In Ratan's view, the fabric of the trusts and philanthropy needed to evolve significantly. The initial phase, from over a century ago, was that of giving individual grants to needy people on grounds of compassion. Thereafter, there was a phase of using funds to also build schools, hospitals or similar institutions that serve society. However, this would also require the edifice to thereafter be run or operated efficiently.

But in the modern age, Ratan felt successful philanthropy lay in making a difference to the quality of lives of people, by helping them sustain their livelihoods and prosperity. This would require appropriate and focused projects to be designed sharply and implemented carefully. Need-based grants to individuals or institutions would also continue alongside these strategic projects.

Under Ratan's overall guidance, the trusts therefore embarked on bold and ambitious projects designed to improve the quality of life in entire regions of the country. A few examples of these projects that came up under his leadership include the Central India initiative, which focused on alleviating poverty and building livelihoods in tribal areas; the Tata water mission, which focused on creating a healthy future for millions of Indians by providing safe, assured and adequate drinking water; and the Himmotthan Pariyojana, undertaken to address the root causes of under-development in the Uttarakhand region.

Ratan Tata urged the team to look at innovative approaches to solving each social problem that the trusts decided to address. Team members recall that the one word that stood out for him was innovation—innovation in thinking, process and implementation to ensure that the most optimal and effective solutions were put in place. In addition, Ratan strongly advocated the leveraging of technology wherever possible, to solve critical challenges. The Tata Trusts also undertook direct implementation of some of these projects, particularly in cases where partner capacity was not readily available.

Innovative partnerships also came to the fore, as part of this strategic approach. One such partnership was a unique project called 'Internet Saathi'. I was quite amazed and also moved when I heard this lovely tale for the first time, way back in 2017. Here is the story.

The year was 2014. Mobile phone and Internet usage had taken off in India. Yet there was a sad truth that faced the country—a huge online gender gap in rural India. Only one in ten Internet users in rural India was a woman. This was a crying shame. Millions of women were being deprived of the multifold, powerful advantages of the Internet just because they did know how to access it.

This is why the Tata Trusts and Google, along with Intel, entered into a partnership called 'Internet Saathi' to impart digital literacy to women in rural India. This was a strategic project with large-scale ambitions, aligned with Ratan Tata's mission for the trusts. The stated goal, announced in 2015, was to reach 3,00,000 villages in the country. This was an astounding target, but if the initiative had to make a real impact, this scale was essential.

'Internet Saathi' was launched in Mumbai on 3 July 2015. Ratan Tata was present at this launch event. Also present were senior representatives from Google and Intel, and officers from Tata Trusts. Inaugurating the event, Ratan said, 'When I was in school, there was no access to even a telephone, and today every rickshaw puller and paan wallah has access to a cellphone. Some of them have also graduated to smartphones. In addition to access, the Internet has brought dignity and self-respect to these people. Google as a company has digitized the world and it is a privilege to work with them towards bringing women online.'

The programme aimed at providing basic training to rural women on the usage of the Internet and its benefits. This would be done by identifying potential women trainers, also called Internet Saathis. These Saathis would receive detailed in-person training. Each Saathi who was selected would also be given two Internet enabled digital devices. These Internet Saathis would then reach around 600 women beneficiaries each, across two to four villages, in a span of six to eight months. They would teach these women how to access the Internet, and also demonstrate specific use-cases.

Tata Trusts focused on smart and agile program management, including the establishment of a foundation called FREND (Foundation for Rural Entrepreneurship Development) for implementation and for developing women entrepreneurs. 'Internet Saathi' scaled rapidly over the next few years. A network of more than 60,000 Saathis was created. By March 2019, over 2.4 crore rural women had been trained in the use of the Internet, across 2,39,000 villages in eighteen states across India.

An impact study conducted in 2018 showed that 70 per cent women accessed the Internet for the first time, through the Internet Saathi programme. Two out of ten rural women trained through this programme went on to start their own business with an average revenue of over Rs 4000 per month. For instance, a woman in a small village began a business making and selling pickles, papads and ladoos, taking orders for these products over the Internet. Another woman learnt bee farming using the Internet and started making honey. She then began using the digital medium to promote her products.

These are just two stories amongst so many, but they illustrate the deep and wide-ranging impact of 'Internet Saathi'. Pause for a moment, and consider how programmes such as this dovetailed with Ratan Tata's objective of helping people sustain their livelihoods and prosperity.

Ratan Tata undertook all these concerted efforts at transforming the Tata Trusts because, in his mind, this was an integral part of his role as chairman of the trusts and as a custodian of the Tata legacy. The trusts have occupied a central position in the Tata group's mission over the past many decades, and ensuring that they were future-ready was therefore, in his mind, totally the right thing to do.

In later years, through the Tata Trusts, Ratan Tata also brought focus to two very important needs of India—

nutrition and cancer care. The story of how he took forward the fight against cancer is narrated in the next chapter, which highlights how he put the nation first in all his efforts.

4

Putting the Nation First

Rarely does the prime minister of India write a full-length article paying tribute to an industrialist. Yet this is exactly what Narendra Modi, the Indian prime minister, did. On 9 November 2024, Prime Minister Modi authored a full-length article that appeared in many Indian newspapers, setting out his thoughts about Ratan Tata, who had passed away exactly a month earlier.

In this article, PM Modi stated, 'He [Ratan Tata] represented the finest traditions of Indian enterprise and a steadfast commitment to the values of integrity, excellence and service.'

He went on to reminisce: "Our close interactions continued when I moved to the centre and he remained a committed partner in our nation-building efforts.'

He then spoke about Ratan Tata's support for the Swachh Bharat Mission and his efforts in healthcare and the fight against cancer in India.

And he ended the article by saying: 'Generations will be grateful to him for making India a better, kinder and more hopeful place.'

This last sentence is very evocative, because this was indeed one of the key drivers of everything Ratan Tata did—he wanted to contribute to the equitable growth and development of India. Speaking in 2004, Ratan once said: 'India is still a developing country, one burdened with enormous inequities. It is our duty to play whatever role we can, in whichever way we can, to diminish those disparities. This is the guiding principle for all of us at Tata.'

Every person I have interviewed for this book has been unanimous that Ratan put the nation first. In the many decisions he took at the helm of the Tata group, I believe that he first asked himself the question: 'Is this good for India?' Only if the answer to this question was yes would he proceed to the next step. For him, what was good for India was good for the Tata group, and that is how he would often decide what was the right thing to do.

I have narrated a few stories below to illustrate how Ratan Tata put the nation first. The fight against cancer, his work as chairman of the Investment Commission of India, his urge to develop the first indigenous Indian car and his response to the communal riots in Mumbai—they all came from this same impulse.

The Fight Against Cancer

The year was 2004. The location was Kolkata. Ratan Tata was addressing the 41st Annual General Meeting of Tata Tea Ltd, in his capacity as chairman of that company. In a meeting that generally discusses business, he announced that the Tata group was examining the setting up of a cancer hospital in Kolkata.

'We feel that we have not done as much as we should have done in the state, and are now considering and examining the setting up of a modern cancer treatment hospital in Kolkata,' he said. He added that this decision was also prompted by the request made by shareholders of Tata Tea, for the company to do something for West Bengal.

Because Ratan Tata believed strongly in equitable growth, he was keen to contribute to reducing disparities between different parts of the country. Therefore, he wanted to do something for Eastern India, including West Bengal—particularly since this region lagged significantly behind other parts of India on many economic indices. This urge would come to the fore time and again in his career—while considering a factory to manufacture the Tata Nano or while establishing hospitals in the north-eastern states.

But now, in 2004, he was focused on creating a world-class, accessible and affordable cancer hospital in Kolkata, to service a region that had seen an increasing incidence of cancer over the past several years. This need had been on Ratan's mind ever since Dr Ketayun Ardeshir Dinshaw, the then director of Tata Memorial Hospital, Mumbai, had mentioned to him that over 25 per cent of all registrations at this cancer hospital came in from patients based in eastern and north-eastern India. However, because of the lack of good treatment facilities in eastern India, many of these patients were forced to travel to Mumbai. The high cost of travel and accommodation in Mumbai often posed a big barrier to their seeking treatment.

For Ratan, Dr Dinshaw's words triggered a call to action. She was a legend in the arena of cancer care in India, having played a pivotal role in shaping the affairs of the Tata Memorial Hospital in Mumbai, India's first cancer hospital, which was also a creation of Tata Trusts, way back in 1940. Ratan now saw an opportunity to contribute to the country by taking forward this legacy to another large region of the country.

His vision for the hospital in Kolkata was very clear: 'Our vision for Tata Medical Centre was an institution that would offer the highest quality cancer treatment laced with compassion and kindness. An institution that would not differentiate between the poor and the affluent when it comes to delivering care.'

The Government of West Bengal provided the land for this charitable cancer hospital at Rajarhat, which was then a fast-developing area of Kolkata. A small project office was immediately established at the Tata Tea headquarters in Kolkata—1, Bishop Lefroy Road. Lakshman Sethuraman, who served as a nodal manager for this hospital project, recalls that this office was initially staffed by two doctors—Dr Sanjay Deka and Dr Brojen Gogoi. Dr Dinshaw of the Tata Memorial Hospital in Mumbai helped steer many of the strategic medical aspects of the project.

Underpinning Ratan Tata on this project was one of his closest associates, a director of Tata Sons and a trustee of Tata Trusts, R.K. Krishna Kumar, a man whose skills in leading new ventures and relentless execution against all odds had been well honed over four long decades of leadership in the Tata group. KK, as he was fondly known to his friends, virtually worked as project manager on this initiative in addition to all his other responsibilities. He kept track of every single move, ably assisted by Lakshman, and he also briefed Ratan Tata from time to time.

Ratan himself got closely involved in many aspects of the project, both functional and aesthetic. One instance of this was when the brand identity and logo design for the Kolkata hospital had to be finalized. A reputed global brand consulting firm, Landor, had agreed to work pro bono on this design. They developed a few designs, of which three were shortlisted by KK. These designs went to Ratan for his views, and he happily made the time.

Ratan had his team paste the three logo designs on cards and put them up in his office. Then, he looked at the logos a few times, quietly contemplated on them and picked out a design that had concentric circles of red and brown dots radiating out from the name of the hospital that had been placed at the centre. 'I feel a lot of hope when I look at this logo, so I have picked it,' he told the team.

Clearly, in his mind, if there was one thing that cancer patients needed, it was hope, and therefore every aspect of the hospital, including the logo, had to convey this. This logo, and the hope that it radiates, continues to be the symbol of the Tata Medical Centre, Kolkata. Tens of thousands of patients would have been greeted by this design of hope between then and now.

Similarly, Ratan, always an architect deep within, wanted to ensure that the most appropriate and durable stone was used for the hospital building. He selected a few options and insisted that a sample wall be created at the site. Thereafter, he visited the location, asked for water to be splashed on this wall to see the impact and only then approved the stone. 'We were waiting with bated breath,' remembers Lakshman, who was present that day on site, 'and eventually when RNT said yes, we were so relieved.' This was the level of detail that Ratan went to, in his pursuit of creating a world-class cancer hospital.

In 2010, Dr Mammen Chandy, who had recently retired from Christian Medical College (CMC) Vellore, was invited to join the Tata Medical Centre, Kolkata, and take charge of the hospital. Dr Chandy, who had pioneered bone marrow treatment in India, was initially sceptical. However a meeting with KK at the Tata group headquarters helped change his mind. Specifically, the fact that his mandate would be to build a hospital with a philanthropic outlook towards patients and not one that was focused on profits appears to have convinced him to take up the opportunity. Dr Chandy thus became the first director of the hospital, and played a splendid role in establishing its firm medical and charitable foundation.

The hospital was formally inaugurated by Ratan Tata on 16 May 2011. His dream of establishing a super-speciality cancer hospital for the people of eastern India had finally come alive, seven years after he had made the first announcement in Kolkata. In a booklet that was published in 2021 to mark ten years of the hospital, Dr Chandy wrote that, as director, his 'single-minded focus was to make cancer treatment affordable. We did not want anyone to turn away from our doors because that person could not afford the treatment.'

He goes on to provide an example of how funds for treatment could be outsourced from organizations with whom the hospital had tied up with.

'For example, today, if an underprivileged girl with thalassemia from a village needs a bone marrow transplant, she can get Rs 10 lakh from Coal India, Rs 5 lakh from the Dorabji Tata Trust, Rs 3 lakh from the PMO fund and Rs 1 lakh from the Chief Minister's Fund. What makes Tata Medical Centre special is that we offer all patients, whether paying or poor, the same experience . . . from the linen to housekeeping and air-conditioning, all patients . . . receive the same protocol.'

In its very first decade, the Tata Medical Centre, Kolkata, began delivering affordable cancer care at scale. Consider these statistics for the first ten years: 12,60,000 patient footfalls. 80,000 in-patient admissions. 35,000 surgeries. 3,27,000 radiology tests. 29,000 nuclear medicine tests. 500 bone marrow transplants. And, most importantly, over 75 per cent of all beds at the hospital earmarked for the underprivileged.

What Dr Chandy and his team were delivering at this cancer hospital was totally in line with Ratan Tata's vision of an institution that does not differentiate between the poor and the affluent. Indeed, this was his vision for healthcare in India.

In 2019, a second phase of the hospital was launched. Between the first and second phase, the cumulative investment was around Rs 800 crore. By any standards, this was a very significant contribution to cancer care in the country.

But for Ratan Tata, this was not enough. In fact, it was just the beginning. As chairman of Tata Trusts, he launched a nationwide cancer care programme in 2017. This programme focuses on a distributed cancer care model, comprising four pillars: (1) access, (2) quality, (3) affordability and (4) awareness, early detection and palliative care. Tata Trusts also began establishing a network of cancer care centres across India, which included day-care centres, onco-pathology laboratories, screening kiosks and hospitals.

Under Ratan's overall guidance, the trusts also began expanding their network of twenty cancer care hospitals across seven states, through collaborations with state governments and other organizations. The states covered included Andhra Pradesh, Assam, Jharkhand, Maharashtra, Uttar Pradesh, Odisha and Gujarat.

In April 2022, Prime Minister Narendra Modi dedicated to the nation seven of these hospitals, all located in Assam. They had been constructed under the auspices of the Assam Cancer Care Foundation, a joint venture of the Assam Government and Tata Trusts. At the same event, the prime minister also laid the foundation of seven new cancer hospitals that would be constructed under the second phase of this project.

Ratan Tata was present at this event, though he looked somewhat frail. In fact, it was one of the last few major public events that Ratan participated in, and also his last big public speech. He began by saying that he could not speak Hindi well, hence he would speak in English. However, during the speech, he could not stop himself from speaking a few sentences in broken Hindi.

As he spoke, he appeared genuinely proud of the many months of advanced thinking and action that had gone into making these cancer hospitals possible in a state where the incidence of cancer was high, but advanced treatment facilities were sorely lacking. He said, 'Today, Assam can tell the world that a small state in India can treat cancer.' He then added, 'I dedicate my final years to healthcare.'

As Prime Minister Modi wrote in his tribute to Ratan Tata, Ratan's efforts 'to make cancer care accessible and affordable were rooted in a profound empathy for those battling diseases, believing that a just society was one that stood by its most vulnerable'. Indeed, the fight against cancer, which Ratan steered selflessly for so many years, was motivated by his desire to put the nation first.

Steel and Solar Panels

In December 2004, the Indian government set up the Investment Commission of India (ICI), with the specific mandate of attracting private and foreign investments. Ratan Tata was appointed chairman of the commission. The other two members were Deepak Parekh and Ashok Sekhar Ganguly, both well-known industrialists.

Ratan Tata accepted this role, notwithstanding his wide-ranging responsibilities as chairman of the Tata group, because he saw the critical importance of investments in driving the growth of the Indian economy. The ICI was given autonomy by the government, with the then finance minister, P. Chidambaram, saying that the commission's advice would be fully backed by the government.

The task ahead was huge. At that time, the foreign direct investment (FDI) into India was a relatively measly $5 billion per year, which was just 1 per cent of the world FDI flows. This also compared very poorly with China, which was already attracting FDI of $60 billion per year at that time. On the other hand, it was estimated that to support an 8 per cent GDP growth of its economy, India would require FDI of at least $72 billion over the next five years. In other words, nearly thrice the existing levels. This was a very ambitious target.

Ratan got down to work quickly on bringing the ICI to life. Regular meetings were scheduled in Bombay House, the headquarters of the Tata group. Reflecting on this, Deepak Parekh has written, 'Those Monday evening meetings when we deliberated and met with investors gave me a true insight into the man (Ratan Tata). Always astute, forthright and clear in his vision for India, he steered the commission to achieve what we did, in often challenging scenarios.'

While Ratan had the support of a full-fledged government department, he also chose to appoint one of his own trusted team members to assist him with the work of the commission, a sort of de-facto secretary. Into this role stepped K.R.S. Jamwal, a young officer of the Tata Administrative Service, who later rose to become the executive director of Tata Industries.

Over twenty years later, Jamwal fondly remembers the work undertaken by Ratan Tata on the Investment Commission. Ratan took up this effort with great urgency and the utmost thoughtfulness, he recalls. Most importantly,

Jamwal recalls that in all this work, Ratan Tata prioritized the needs of the nation well above the needs of the Tata group. In fact, even if in some cases the national need was likely to somewhat disadvantage the Tatas, Ratan would always put the nation first.

One such story concerns the efforts made to bring in investment into the metals and mining sector of the Indian economy. POSCO (formerly Pohang Iron and Steel Company), a South Korean firm, which is also one of the world's largest steel manufacturing companies, was exploring a proposal to establish a new steel plant in Odisha, in India. The South Korean costs were too high to support a wide range of steel-making activities, and therefore POSCO was seeking to establish a base in India.

Early in his tenure as chairman, Ratan Tata met Finance Minister P. Chidambaram to discuss various subjects relating to the commission. Jamwal was present at this meeting and recalls that much of the time was spent discussing the POSCO steel plant investment proposal. What was proposed was a very large steel plant, with a capacity of 12 million metric tons (MMT) per annum. This could well turn out to be the biggest FDI proposal for the country.

Mr Tata stressed, from this first discussion itself, that POSCO would need a lot of help and support, to navigate the complexities of doing business and setting up a new plant in India. POSCO was a very successful steel company, but it had no prior experience of walking through the Indian maze. Potential issues ranged from land acquisition to port and road connectivity to environmental impact assessment. Equally importantly, POSCO and the state government of Odisha had to build a rapport with each other, to ensure smooth progress of the project.

What was, however, clear to all concerned was that the POSCO project, if it came in, would be a direct competitor to Tata Steel. While this was well before Tata Steel's new plant in Kalinganagar, Odisha, had come up, there was no running away from the fact that a very efficient global competitor setting up base in the country would result in formidable competition to Tata Steel, one of the oldest and most prominent flagship businesses of the Tata group.

Ratan Tata addressed this thorny issue upfront. His view, recalls Jamwal, was that the POSCO investment was a very good thing for India. Yes, it would create more competition for Tata Steel, but national interest came first. He was therefore genuinely very supportive of the POSCO project. This was not mere lip service. Ratan advised Jamwal to help POSCO on anything that they needed, starting with economic impact assessments by the right agencies to help them get a good on-ground view and navigate local issues that arise in virtually every large project. Even within the Tata group, the clear message was that Ratan Tata was encouraging of the POSCO project, because it was good for the country. There was no second or different point of view, either in his meetings at Tata Steel or elsewhere.

'Ratan Tata was very open and transparent with us,' says Jamwal. 'His views were known clearly to us. In fact, his office and he used to even share his calendar, every single appointment, with his small team, including me, so that we could plan our work accordingly. His life was an open book to his team. On this particular project, he was clear that he would help POSCO in every way possible.'

Therefore, when Finance Minister Chidambaram requested Ratan Tata to meet the chief minister of Odisha and sensitize him to all the needs of the project, Ratan agreed to do so immediately. Ratan, accompanied by the two other members of the Investment Commission, went down to Bhubaneshwar to meet with Chief Minister Naveen Patnaik.

At a meeting that lasted more than half a day, Ratan Tata had the opportunity to discuss the POSCO project in detail with the chief minister and some of his senior bureaucrats. Ratan emphasized the importance of this project to the nation and the state, and put forward his views on some of the key steps that would help take it to fruition. For instance, the state government's support for ensuring that locals impacted by the project understood the benefits of such a mega-project in terms of jobs and economic activity would be very important. Thereafter, the state government's help would be critical in relocation of families impacted by the land acquisition. Ratan also highlighted that POSCO required guidance and support in taking forward various elements of the project.

In June 2005, after many discussions, POSCO signed a Memorandum of Understanding with the Government of Odisha to implement this huge steel plant project. This attracted immediate global attention for being the biggest FDI in India at that time—an investment estimated at $12 billion. While the term of the ICI headed by Ratan Tata ended in December 2009, the efforts to implement this mega project continued well beyond that time, but perhaps the challenges were too many or not adequately addressed. Despite the best efforts of the state government, the project ran into significant public resistance, with villagers opposing acquisition of their lands, as well as other regulatory hurdles. Eventually, in 2017, POSCO exited the project.

Interestingly, several years later, in October 2024, POSCO and the JSW Group of India announced that they had signed a memorandum of understanding to develop an integrated mega steel plant in India. If Ratan Tata had been alive, I think he would have personally been very happy to see this new development, notwithstanding the fact that the JSW Group is a key competitor to Tata Steel.

What stands out to me in this story is Ratan Tata's absolute support to a project that was good for India, despite the fact that it would create formidable competition for the Tata group.

Yet another small but equally revealing story of Ratan putting the nation above the company or the industry sector comes from the space of solar energy. This happened around 2009, when Ratan Tata was co-chair of the US-India CEO Forum. Preparatory to a session of this forum, he met with Montek Singh Ahluwalia, at that time the deputy chairman of the Planning Commission of India.

Jamwal, who was assisting Ratan Tata at that time, has narrated this story to me.

The conversation between Ratan and Montek veered briefly from US-India CEO Forum-related matters to the subject of solar panels. It was a subject that Ratan was familiar with, particularly since the Tata group had a presence in this industry through Tata BP Solar, a joint venture company that had been established in 1989.

There was a discussion on whether China was dumping their solar panels into India. 'Dumping' is a term used in international trade to indicate that a country or company is exporting a product at a lower price than in the home market. Often, 'dumping' implies that the product is being exported even lower than the cost of production.

Montek said that the government would perhaps have to consider some kind of protection to the domestic solar panels manufacturing industry, to safeguard it from these cheap Chinese solar panels entering India. Montek would perhaps have expected instant support for this stance from Ratan Tata, a captain of the Indian industry.

Ratan, on the other hand, had a completely different point of view. He turned to Montek and said, 'If we get cheap solar panels from China, we generate cheap solar electricity in India, which is good for our country.' In other words, he was not supportive of a tariff barrier against these Chinese solar panels, which would increase their price and consequently increase the cost of generating solar electricity in India.

What about the protection of domestic industry? To this, Ratan said, 'Our domestic Indian industry has to learn how to compete.'

Ratan said this quite categorically because his own prior research had shown that the actual cost of production of solar panels in China was truly much lower than the cost at which they were being manufactured in India. This was therefore not a case of unfair subsidization, but one of actual cost efficiency, and Indian industry had to learn to become equally cost competitive.

Once again, the interests of the country—cheaper electricity for customers—took higher priority in Ratan Tata's mind than the narrower interests of the solar panels manufacturing sector. For him, quite instinctively, the nation came first.

India's First Indigenous Car

In 1993, Ratan Tata, the chairman of the Tata group and Tata Motors, addressed the Automobile Component Manufacturers' Association of India in New Delhi. On this platform, he suggested the possibility of component and car manufacturers in India getting together to produce an indigenous Indian car. His intent was to emulate the Japanese and deliver a project that would make the nation proud.

After all, cars have always been symbols of patriotism and pride. Consider examples such as Toyota and Japan, Hyundai and Korea, General Motors and the USA, Mercedes-Benz and Germany, Jaguar Land Rover and the UK, and Fiat and Italy. Why should India, which had already put a satellite into space by then, not have its own car?

What was the reaction to Ratan Tata's address and clarion call? He reflected on this several years later:

'Needless to say, there was considerable criticism and cynicism about my suggestion. In the absence of a positive reaction, I decided that if we were not going to do this as a collaborative national effort, Tata Motors would undertake the lead effort. In 1995, we formally undertook a programme to develop a new Indian car. Two types of reactions were forthcoming at that stage: one was that we were being very brave, but the other, which came more often, was that we were being very foolish.'

Notwithstanding such scepticism from many quarters, Ratan Tata was determined to go ahead and give India its first indigenous car. With his team at Tata Motors, he began crafting the vision for this car. In his own words:

'We started out to design an Indian car from scratch. We felt that the Ambassador, much as it is maligned, is the ideal size for the travelling Indian public. So we decided to design a car with the internal volume of an Ambassador, the size of a Maruti Zen, and the ease of entering and exiting, particularly for the rear seats. We thought of pricing it close to Maruti 800, which is a very successful car, and adding the economy of diesel. Finally, we packaged this into a contemporary design.'

This was a very ambitious project, and one without precedent in the country. An indigenous car would involve a design created specifically for India, it would entail developing over 3000 discrete components within the country, and then manufacturing and assembly. It was also a very expensive venture, entailing investments of more than Rs 1700 crore, which could make or break the company's fortunes.

Ratan did not balk at these figures, because this was one of his dreams for India. He also believed that Tata Motors had the innate capability to make this a success, though the company had never before made passenger cars. He gave the project his go-ahead, and a passionate team at Tata Motors thereafter immersed itself in the creation of India's first indigenous car.

Ratan personally championed the project. Over the next few years, many milestones were accomplished under his leadership.

A futuristic design for the car was developed, the likes of which had never been seen before in India. This task was entrusted by Ratan to the Engineering Research Centre (ERC) of Tata Motors in Pune. The designs were evolved and finalized in collaboration with a famous Turin-based design house, I.DE.A. Ratan insisted on a design that leapfrogged into the future and therefore advised that design work be undertaken in Europe, which was way ahead of India at that time. His objective—a car that was ahead of its time. When the eventual design was unveiled, the reaction everywhere was a 'Wow'.

The engineering design process was completely automated at the ERC using computer-aided design (CAD) and computer-aided manufacturing, both of which were a novelty in those years. Tata Motors invested over Rs 120 crore on 225 CAD stations for its 340 engineers to work on.

The car was named Tata Indica. The name Indica said it all. This was how the ancient Greeks referred to India, and this car was, in its essence, all about Indian pride.

For the 3885 discrete parts that would go into the Indica, there was a sharp focus on either manufacturing in-house or developing local vendors. No efforts were spared to ensure that these components were world-class. For many sophisticated components, joint ventures were created, under the umbrella of a company called Tata Auto Components Ltd (TACO). For instance, for manufacturing car seats, a joint venture was established with Johnson Controls of the USA. In addition, over 300 local vendors were successfully developed within a relatively short span of time.

Manufacturing a new car would have typically cost not less than $2 billion, which was unaffordable for Tata Motors at that time. Ratan Tata and his leadership team navigated this huge challenge by taking a road less travelled, and made the Indica car project possible within $400 million. They did this because they identified a disused Nissan manufacturing plant in Australia, negotiated and purchased it for one-sixth of what a new plant would have cost, dismantled the plant (all 14,800 tonnes of machinery), shipped it to India and then reassembled it in Pune, added some more new equipment, and thus created a cost-effective manufacturing plant for the new car.

Ratan Tata regularly reviewed the progress of the project and also visited the Tata Indica factory in Pune several times during the development stage. He met with workers during his visits, stopping by quite often to exchange a few words and encourage them.

In 1998, the first Tata Indica rolled out of the Tata Motors facility in Pune. The reaction to the overall design, space and affordability of the car was a huge 'Wow'. Here was the first-ever passenger car developed and manufactured indigenously in India, and it had all the looks of a world-class vehicle. The car garnered a handsome 1,15,000 fully paid bookings within eight days of its launch.

Almost immediately thereafter, Tata Indica ran into initial quality issues. Customers who had bought the first version of the Indica called in, complaining of high noise and vibration levels. Performance of the engine also came in for criticism. Word of mouth quickly turned from positive to negative. The competition became hyperactive and began writing premature epitaphs for Indica. A constant refrain in those days was: Had Ratan Tata made a big mistake in attempting to launch India's first indigenous car?

Ratan Tata was unfazed by these critics. He once again led from the forefront, to have these quality issues resolved. At an emergency meeting, he encouraged his team members to vent their views of what had gone wrong, before directing the meeting towards the actions required.

For the immediate term, 'retrofit camps' were organized, where 45,000 Indica cars were repaired, with forty-two parts being replaced entirely at the company's cost. In the meanwhile, working on a war footing, the engineers of Tata Motors made the design changes required to eliminate the quality issues that had surfaced. A new robust version of the car, named Indica V2, was ready by 2001, where key quality problems had been completely eliminated.

The impact of the Indica V2 was extraordinary and immediate. It became the fastest-selling automobile in Indian history when it completed sales of 1,00,000 cars in less than eighteen months. The 2003 JD Power India customer satisfaction survey, an independent and widely respected review of cars, ranked the Indica diesel car as the best in the operating costs category, even ahead of the market leader, Maruti 800. The reputed television programme *BBC Wheels* declared Indica 'the best car in the Rs 3 lakh to Rs 5 lakh price category'. The confidence was back, and India's first indigenous passenger car was going from strength to strength.

The Tata Indica transformed Tata Motors from a successful maker of commercial vehicles to a modern automobile company. Today, Tata Motors has an amazing line-up of cars and SUVs that enjoy great consumer franchise. In 2024, the year in which Ratan Tata passed away, the Tata Punch was the largest-selling car in India, having taken this pole position away from Maruti Suzuki, the market leader.

Perhaps even more importantly, Ratan Tata's move to launch an indigenous passenger car served as a catalyst for transforming the car industry in India. It established a very successful supply chain for the indigenous design and manufacture of cars by developing a range of competent local vendors, some of whom also had collaborations with the best names in the world. It re-established Indian pride in engineering and manufacturing. By making India one of the few countries globally to produce its own indigenous car, it emphasized that the engineering sector in the country was alive, vibrant and kicking.

Most significantly, Tata Indica became a symbol of Indian prowess and pride. What Ratan Tata and his team had delivered here was yet another pioneering venture for the nation, going where no other Indian company had gone before.

Here are some thoughts that Ratan Tata expressed, while speaking about the Tata Indica:

'Can we do something that has never been done before? I would like to believe that it can be done. We can make it happen. We just need to make sure that we do it.

'It is important, particularly for the younger people in India, to believe in what we are doing and that we can do much more. I hope the younger generation will take India to new heights, which I am sure they can. They need to believe in and recognize the potential of their own capabilities.'

These observations provide us a glimpse into why Ratan Tata thought that he was doing the right thing by creating the first truly indigenous Indian car.

Bombay Is Not for Burning

The city of Bombay (the official name of Mumbai was still Bombay in those days) was torn apart by riots during December 1992 and January 1993. This was in the immediate aftermath of the demolition of the Babri Masjid in Ayodhya.

The riots racked the city and thousands fled in fear. In one of the biggest tragedies ever to strike the financial capital of India, over 900 people lost their lives. The city, long known for its cosmopolitan and liberal outlook, was suddenly engulfed in waves of mob rioting and communal violence. The city stared into the abyss, and there were scenes of destruction all around.

For Ratan Tata, Bombay was his beloved home. He had grown up in this city and had gone to school here. This was the city that had nurtured the Tata group for over a century. Now, as chairman of the Tata group, he was one of the foremost citizens of Bombay.

The riots devastated Ratan. He was not just disturbed, he felt compelled to do what best he could to help.

And therefore, on 19 January 1993, he published in the *Times of India* an advertisement that contained an open letter written by him. This letter was written in his personal capacity, and he paid from his personal funds for the publication of the advertisement.

In his hard-hitting letter, Ratan spoke about how the people of Bombay had always lived in harmony, in a city primarily driven by industry, opportunity and enterprise. He called out the 'marauding mobs of frenzied hooligans, allegedly unleased by political war lords' because of whom large areas of the city were under siege. He spoke about the real citizens of Bombay—the people who had protected their friends and neighbours from the mobs. He then urged all citizens of Bombay to stand together and 'stop being silent spectators in the destruction of the city and the killing of neighbours by those who thrive on fear and chaos'.

Ratan ended his open letter with these powerful words: 'Bombay is not for burning.' The letter was signed: 'Ratan N. Tata. A concerned citizen'.

In publishing this open letter, Ratan Tata chose to leave the safety of his corner office in Bombay House and corporate boardrooms. He did this because he believed that harmony was the most important and urgent objective at the time, and he wanted to contribute to this goal in whatever manner he could. Later, he also deposed before the Srikrishna Commission, which was investigating the causes of these riots. He would have known that an open letter such as this, with its references to political war lords, and thereafter his frank deposition, would not have been perceived kindly by some powerful people. And yet he took a public posture on this subject because he thought this was the right thing to do.

This was Ratan Tata. He acted according to his conscience and he always put the nation—and in this case the city—first. These strong instincts would come to the fore once again when terrorists attacked Mumbai, including the Taj Mahal Palace Hotel, sixteen years later, in 2008, a story that is narrated later in this book.

5

Ethical Conduct of Business

For Ratan Tata, following the ethics of business was non-negotiable, and it was central to 'doing the right thing'.

Ratan understood that this was challenging, particularly in a country like India, where corruption and political proximity, which comes with its own strings attached, have been known to deliver results. Yet, from every single episode I have seen and heard, he did not budge from this principle, thereby ensuring that the business he was in charge of was conducted without compromise to the highest standards of ethics.

Ratan defined what the ethical conduct of business meant to the Tata group and to him in a brief sentence that he wrote in the epilogue to the book *The Creation of Wealth*, which I have referred to earlier but repeat here because it stands out for its clarity. Here is what he said about what it means: 'a great value system and uncompromising in its goal to achieve results without partaking in corruption, bribery and/or political influence.'

To him, the ethical standards established by his predecessors, including Jamsetji Tata and J.R.D. Tata, were the most important assets of the Tata group. This was at the core of why the Tata group enjoyed trust from all their stakeholders.

In an interview with the in-house magazine *Tata Review* in 2012, Ratan goes on to elaborate this view: 'I have said this before and I continue to say it today—the most valuable asset we have in our group is our ethical standards and our values ... we have managed to grow and we have managed to abide by our values without compromising. We have been respected for that and, in some cases, we may have lost opportunities due to that. But, as I have frequently said, I can go to bed at night knowing that I did not succumb.'

This last line—'I can go to bed at night knowing that I did not succumb'—has always struck me as being particularly powerful. It highlights why the ethical conduct of business is important not only to value-based corporations but also to the individuals who run them.

While the Tata group has always been known to stand for the highest ethical standards, Ratan Tata institutionalized this code of honour for the first time ever in the group's history by putting in place a written 'Tata Code of Conduct' (TCOC) in 1998. This document, which remains a bedrock of the group's functioning until today, highlights the principles of ethics, integrity and transparency that govern the manner in which Tata companies and their employees are expected to conduct themselves.

Many of us in the Tata group refer to this document by its acronym: TCOC. A detailed ethics structure across the companies of the group ensures that the TCOC is implemented in letter and spirit across more than one million Tata employees and tens of thousands of business partners. Apart from regular training sessions on these guidelines, an annual Ethics Conclave is held where leaders of the group participate in discussing emerging areas and dilemmas candidly. From all that I have seen over my long tenure in the Tata group, ethical violations are addressed firmly, through a well-structured ethics organization that cuts across the companies of the group. This structure and process have emerged from the TCOC that Ratan Tata put in place.

What Ratan also did, most importantly, was to walk the talk on business ethics. In this chapter, I narrate a few stories which bring to life this moral compass of a leader who 'did not succumb'.

The Airline Saga

On 15 November 2010, Ratan Tata delivered a keynote address in Dehradun to mark the tenth foundation day of the state of Uttarakhand. His lecture was titled 'India in the 21st Century: Opportunities and Challenges'.

Following the lecture, he participated in an interactive session where members of the media were also present. During this interaction, he spoke about his experiences from around a decade earlier, when the Tata group had applied more than once to start an airline in India, but had unfortunately not got the approvals required.

'Many of you may know through the media that we had enormous problems. We went through three governments, three prime ministers. And each time there was a particular individual that thwarted our efforts to form another airline.'

The context here was that the Tata group, under Ratan Tata's leadership, had tried not once but thrice over a period of five years to launch a domestic airline or re-enter the field of aviation. These efforts had happened in 1995, when the Government of India was led by Prime Minister Narasimha Rao; in 1997, when the government was led by H.D. Deve Gowda; and in 2000, when the government was led by Atal Bihari Vajpayee.

In all three instances, the group had run into opposition and many problems, and the attempts had been unsuccessful. These attempts, and what derailed them, have been written about widely and have also been narrated in the excellent book *The Tata Group: From Torchbearers to Trailblazers,* authored by Shashank Shah. An insider's view of some related events is also available in the book *An Outsider Everywhere: Revelations by an Insider,* written by M.K. Kaw, who was secretary of civil aviation in the Government of India during 1997–98. For the sake of brevity, I will not go into all these details here.

These were the futile attempts through 'three governments, three prime ministers' that Ratan Tata was referring to during his interaction at Dehradun. While Ratan Tata did not name the individual who had thwarted the Tata group's efforts in all these three instances, it was quite clear that he was referring to vested interests at work.

Ratan went on to relate the following incident:

'So I happened to be on a flight once and a fellow industrialist was seated next to me. And he said, "I don't understand. You people are very stupid. You know the minister wants Rs 15 crore. So why don't you pay it? You want the airline."'

Ratan went on to say that he responded to that industrialist, 'You can't understand it. I just want to go to bed at night knowing that I haven't got the airline by paying for it.'

For Ratan, doing what that industrialist had suggested was unthinkable.

Just to be clear, the Tata group clarified through a statement later that day: 'No minister ever asked Mr Tata for a bribe. The fellow industrialist expressed his personal viewpoint that some minister was asking for a bribe. Mr Tata in no way was in agreement to the fact that he was asked for a bribe by any minister.'

Nonetheless, Ratan Tata's spontaneous response to what the fellow industrialist told him is a clear indication of his firm views on the subject—he would rather lose a business opportunity than gain it through unethical means. Whether it be in aviation or any other industry.

There is, however, a happy postscript to this aviation story. In 2020, the Government of India decided to completely privatize Air India by divesting 100 per cent of its stake in the airline. The Tata group was one of two bidders who qualified. The Tata Sons bid was led this time by N. Chandrasekaran, Ratan Tata's successor as chairman. In October 2021, Tata Sons emerged as the winner in this clear and transparent bidding process. In January 2022, Air India came back to the Tata group.

Ratan Tata's response to this homecoming, which indicated his great happiness, was 'Welcome back, Air India!'

Progressive Electoral Trust

Corporate funding to political parties was an opaque space in India for several decades. Many companies would leverage their financial strength to extract favours from the political parties in power. Conversely, some political parties would also pressurize companies to contribute to their coffers, with explicit or implicit rewards and threats being held out. Unaccounted black money would change hands in some of these transactions. And because political parties were inevitably in need of money to help them fight various elections, this cycle continued, year after year, without pause. Funding of political parties thus became a fertile ground for black money, favour-seeking, extortion and other corrupt practices.

Soon after Ratan Tata became chairman of the Tata group, he mentioned to some of his colleagues that he would want to protect himself and Tata companies from such ad hoc political pressures by introducing a fair and transparent system of funding political parties for elections. Elections constitute the foundation of democracy, and any such equitable funding system would, in effect, be a contribution of the Tata group towards strengthening democracy in India. In addition, if a fair and transparent system of funding political parties could be evolved, which both Tata companies and other corporates could participate in, this would be a very good step towards bringing ethics into a space which had always displayed many shades of black and grey.

Ratan Tata took up this subject on priority, recalls Farokh Subedar, a Tata group veteran, who later rose to become the COO of Tata Sons. This was a matter without precedent, and something well beyond the usual remit of business. Hence, it needed new thinking and thoughtful formulation. Ratan requested Dinesh Vyas, an eminent senior advocate, who was an independent tax counsel for several Tata entities, to help him with this initiative.

As they studied political funding in various parts of the world, they came upon a good model which was in use in Germany. Here, funds are allocated to political parties transparently, with one key criterion being their success in an election. In other words, parties receive a specified amount for every vote that is cast in their favour. This triggered the thought: Why not apply a similar transparent model to the Tata group's funding of political parties for elections?

Based on this principle, Ratan Tata established the Electoral Trust in 1996 to make donations to political parties. His clear objective in doing this was to drive transparency, fairness and accountability in corporate funding of political parties, as well as to discourage corruption and favour-seeking. If any political party now approached Ratan for a donation, he could tell them that there was a clear structure and process, and that the Trust would distribute money in line with this process.

By any standards, this was a pioneering move designed to strengthen ethics in business, while supporting Indian democracy. In fact, seventeen years later in 2013, when the Government of India introduced a similar scheme—called the Electoral Trusts Scheme 2013—it was quite similar to the one that Ratan had put in place. Quite interestingly, at this point, the entity created by Ratan Tata and the Tata group, which had been simply named Electoral Trust at the time of its formation in 1996, had to be renamed the Progressive Electoral Trust since its original name had been taken over by the government scheme!

While Ratan was the champion of the Progressive Electoral Trust, he wanted it to be managed by an independent panel of trustees to ensure complete objectivity. Dinesh Vyas was appointed its president. All companies of the Tata group were free to contribute, and the Trust also welcomed contributions by other non-Tata corporates. Hence, Ratan decided that the Trust should not carry the Tata name, since it was open to all.

Contributions to political parties would be made as per a well-defined formula that was based on the vote share obtained by each party. Therefore, trustees would have no discretion to decide which parties to fund or how much to fund each party. By removing human discretion from a subject where different humans could have very different views, and instead basing fund allocation on vote share data, objective fairness was achieved. In essence, it was the voice of the public and not the voice of Tata directors or trustees that determined how much funding each political party would receive.

At the time the Progressive Electoral Trust was created by Ratan Tata, there was no specific law in India that dealt with electoral trusts. Hence, an optimal structure was created which was compliant with the existing laws of the land. It was also decided that the Trust would fund political parties in the year of the national Lok Sabha elections, and that it would steer clear of state elections.

Even as Ratan put in place this mechanism to help corporates make political funding in a non-corrupt and transparent manner, an interesting issue came up that pertained to taxation. Farokh Subedar, who worked closely with Ratan Tata on this initiative, recalls that his taxation colleagues in various Tata companies soon began approaching him with the question: Could their companies claim tax deductions for the funds they had contributed to the Trust, and which the Trust had in turn contributed to political parties?

Because there was no specific law in place pertaining to the Electoral Trust, there was no clear answer to this question. Farokh decided to take this matter up to Ratan Tata for his advice, after obtaining some expert views. He took the opinion of legal and tax experts, drafted out a memo based on their interpretations, and tabled this to Ratan for his consideration. Farokh recalls that meeting vividly even today, thirty years later.

Ratan Tata read the memo, understood the matter, then turned to Farokh immediately and said, 'I have not set up this Trust to get tax deductions. This is our contribution to democracy, and if we have to suffer a tax disallowance, we will suffer it. Therefore, please instruct all these taxation managers not to claim the tax deduction.'

Farokh remembers that Ratan Tata said this spontaneously and without any hesitation. In other words, he was not interested in pursuing the legal nuances of the matter, or seeing whether the tax deduction could perhaps be claimed through some legal interpretation, because in his mind the purpose of the Electoral Trust was very clear. It was to strengthen democracy through transparency, without expecting any other return, not even a tax deduction.

He also recalls that Ratan wrote down his views as a noting on the margins of that same memo—this was a pink memo that was widely used at the Tata group headquarters in the days before the start of the digital era.

That was, however, not the end of the story. A few years later, a law came into place explicitly mentioning that contributions made by electoral trusts would be eligible for tax deduction under the provisions of income tax. So Farokh Subedar took this matter back to Ratan Tata, and once again sought his advice. Farokh also reminded Ratan that he (Ratan) had specifically advised him (Farokh), a few years ago, that Tata companies should not claim the tax deduction against these contributions.

Ratan Tata considered the matter, turned to Farokh and said, 'I well recall instructing you that our companies should not attempt to claim a tax deduction. But that was when the law did not explicitly so permit such a tax deduction. Who am I to stop my companies from claiming a tax deduction if the law now specifically permits them to do so? If the law says that they can claim a deduction for their contributions, then yes, they should do that. That becomes their duty.'

Ratan went on to say, 'When there was no law governing this subject, I expressed my personal view. There was no

(Courtesy of Tata Central Archives)

A profile of Ratan Tata. His eyes were sharp, and he spoke thoughtfully, slowly and clearly. This is how I will always remember him.

(Courtesy of Tata Central Archives)

Three legends in one frame. Ratan Tata with his mentor J.R.D. Tata, in front of the statue of Jamsetji Tata at Tata Steel, Jamshedpur. Ratan considered himself a custodian of the Tata legacy, which has its roots in Jamsetji Tata's vision and philosophy.

(Courtesy of Tata Steel)

Ratan Tata meeting employees of Tata Steel during a visit to Jamshedpur. Care and compassion for people was at the heart of his leadership.

(Courtesy of Tata Motors)

Ratan Tata drives the first Tata Indica off the assembly line in the Tata Motors plant in Pune in 1998. For him, the Indica was a great feeling of national achievement.

Ratan Tata with colleagues at the Tata Trusts Small Animal Hospital in Mumbai. The hospital was one of his cherished pet projects. It was inaugurated in July 2024, just three months before he passed away.

Ratan Tata speaking at the re-opening of the Taj Mahal Tower wing on 21 December 2008, less than a month after it was attacked by terrorists on 26 November 2008. In an emotional but defiant address, he said, 'We can be hurt but we cannot be knocked down.'

(Courtesy of Tata Motors)

Two icons of our age—Ratan Tata in a conversation with President APJ Abdul Kalam.

(Courtesy of Tata Steel)

Ratan Tata enjoying a happy moment with N. Chandrasekaran, chairman, Tata Sons, at Jamshedpur. In the background is a bust of Jamsetji Tata, founder of the Tata group.

(Courtesy of Shantanu Naidu)

Ratan Tata with his canine friend, Goa. Goa would walk across to Ratan's office and sit there with him. Ratan also had a small bed made for Goa in the conference room.

(Courtesy of Tata Business Excellence Group)

Ratan Tata addressing the JRD-QV Awards event in 2011. He instituted the JRD-QV Awards to evangelize excellence in all spheres of business across the Tata group.

(Courtesy of Tata Business Excellence Group)

Ratan Tata with the Titan watches team, which won the Sustained Business Excellence Award at the JRD-QV event in 2009. This was a proud moment for the author, who was at that time the chief operating officer of the Titan watches business.

(Courtesy of Tata Motors)

Ratan Tata at the unveiling of the Tata Nano in 2008. The Nano was one of his most audacious dreams.

(Courtesy of Atul Bhide)

Ratan Tata recording the foreword for the audio autobiography of Dr Verghese Kurien at the boardroom of Bombay House. Despite a hectic schedule, he met his commitment to Atul Bhide, who had requested him for this recording.

(Courtesy of the author)

The bust of Ratan Tata at Bombay House, the global headquarters of the Tata group. Each time I pass by this bust, I offer a small prayer to this leader who has been a source of inspiration to millions of people, including myself.

(Courtesy of Sadiq Basha M.)

The author with Ratan Tata. What could I say to a man who has inspired an entire nation? This book is my tribute and an attempt to learn from him.

law, so that was a moral decision. But now, when there is a specific law, we should go as per that law.'

He added, 'I cannot put my companies in a worse off situation today just because I had said a few years ago that we cannot claim a tax deduction. The law has kept pace, and now it is explicit enough for me to change my view.'

Farokh Subedar then advised the participating Tata companies that they could claim a tax deduction on their contributions, as now permitted by the law.

Reflecting on this episode, Farokh says, 'It is very interesting the way Ratan Tata's mind worked. In his mind, after due thought, there was a definite sense of what was right. He said and did what he thought was right.'

Ratan Tata's decision to form the Electoral Trust to build transparency into the political funding process, as well as his views on the taxation matter referred to above, reflect his commitment to the highest standard of ethics in the conduct of business. For him, both these decisions were all about doing the right thing.

A Matter of Mines and More

Over the past few decades, the mining sector in India has been at the centre of several corruption scams. These scandals have typically involved politicians, bureaucrats, businessmen and other power brokers.

Tata Steel has had more than a century of experience in mining raw materials that are used for its steel-making operations, with many of its mining licences going back to the early 1900s when the company was founded. The company stands committed to responsible mining practices and taking forward its mining operations in an ethical manner, in keeping with the Tata code of conduct.

Ratan Tata served as chairman of Tata Steel during most of his tenure as head of the Tata group. Indeed, Tata Steel has always been a flagship company of the Tatas, and the chairman of the group has also typically been at the helm of this company. Therefore, from time to time, he also had to answer questions relating to the company's mining operations.

In 2010, Ratan was interviewed by the Indian television channel NDTV on a range of topics. The interviewer was the well-known journalist, Shekhar Gupta.

During the course of this conversation, Ratan Tata was asked whether 'you sometimes pay if you have to pay'. Ratan Tata was categorical in his response: 'We've never done so. Never.'

Later in the interview, Shekhar Gupta went on to ask: 'And you have never done it even for a mining lease anywhere? Because now it is considered to be the normal thing for mining leases.'

Ratan Tata responded to him definitively, saying: 'No, it is not . . . on our part, no.'

When Shekhar Gupta queried him further whether the Tatas had suffered because of that, Ratan responded that the Tatas had several mining leases that were still not extended.

That was Ratan Tata's consistent stance on all matters, including mining. He would never consider or permit corruption or bribery. It did not matter to him at all if this uncompromising stance led to a significant economic loss for the company.

When Ratan Tata was the chairman of Tata Steel, Dr J.J. Irani had been the managing director of the company for several years. His memoirs, titled *Doctor Steel*, contain many interesting stories. There is a reference to mining as well, in the introductory chapter of this book. It says:

'According to Dr Irani, on one occasion, Tata Steel even lost a mine right worth hundreds of crores, because it did not budge from its core principles of doing fair and honest business.'

Ishaat Hussain, who was the CFO of Tata Steel at that time, also shared an interesting story with me in this context.

Once, soon after Tata Steel had lost some mining rights, Ratan Tata travelled to a mining location of Tata Steel. There, he held an open house with the employees. Some of the employees wanted to know: Was there no way in which Tata Steel could have got an extension of the lease for these mines which had not been renewed?

Ratan Tata is reported to have responded: 'Will you please specify what could have been the way?'

He then went on to say: 'Either you are ethical or you are not ethical. You cannot pick and choose as to what you will be ethical about.'

He also said: 'Once you breach this principle, then there is no end to it. Where do you stop?'

This was an expression of Ratan's strong belief that if ethics were breached, the organization would begin corroding over time and eventually collapse. He was also clear that he would not permit this to happen in the Tata group.

Ishaat Hussain recalled that even at shareholders' meetings, when such questions were put to Ratan, he would respond: 'These are my principles, these are the values of the group. If you don't think that what I have done is right, then you can vote with your feet. You can sell your shares, or you can change me.' So for him, there was no compromise on the issue of ethics.

Ratan also wrote: 'I hope the future generations in Tatas will recognize these traditions as being critical to the fabric and the fundamentals on which our group was built and grew so successfully for over a century.'

For Ratan Tata, ethics in business was not just another dimension of 'doing the right thing'. It was the fundamental pillar on which everything else stood.

6

Beyond Legal Compliance: Being Morally Correct

For Ratan Tata, abiding by the law was essential. But far more important was being morally correct, even if this meant going well beyond legal compliance.

In 2009, reflecting on the Tata group's code of honour in an in-house publication, Ratan Tata wrote that the multitude of initiatives which Tata companies had sowed and fostered from their earliest days flow from a wellspring of voluntary, as opposed to obligatory, commitment. He mentioned that these could be initiatives across the spectrum, including employee relations, ethical governance, environment or community causes.

Specifically, he pointed out that Jamsetji Tata, the founder of the group, his sons Dorabji Tata and Ratanji Tata and, subsequently, J.R.D. Tata, embodied the same values in their corporate actions.

Perhaps one powerful historical instance of this that may have been on Ratan's mind was how Dorabji Tata, the second chairman of the Tata group, had dealt with a very challenging situation in Tata Steel. In 1924, the company was on the verge of shutting down because of difficult business conditions. Dorabji received a telegram from the steel plant in Jamshedpur informing him that there was no money to pay wages. Dorabji Tata and his wife, Meherbai, pledged their entire personal wealth of around Rs 1 crore to raise a loan from the Imperial Bank of India. Using the funds raised from this loan, Tata Steel paid wages and continued its steel-making operations. Within a few years, the business environment had taken a turn for the better, and the company began prospering once again. Over a century later, today, Tata Steel remains a proud and prosperous company.

There was no legal requirement for Dorabji Tata to pledge his personal wealth to save Tata Steel, a publicly listed company. Yet he did this of his own volition, because he believed that this was the honourable thing to do. And in doing so, he saved Tata Steel.

For Ratan Tata, this very same spirit of being morally correct was integral to 'doing the right thing' in every situation. R.K. Krishna Kumar, a Tata veteran, who rose to become a director of Tata Sons, worked very closely with Ratan for several years. He has written, 'Once he [Ratan] accepts what is the ethical position in a situation, he becomes inflexible and accepts no compromise, no matter what the consequences. That kind of a firm moral commitment in the world of business is quite extraordinary.'

In this chapter, I will narrate a few stories that illustrate how Ratan Tata went beyond legal compliance to do what he thought was morally correct.

A Crisis at Tata Finance

In 2001, a shocking letter landed up on Ratan Tata's table. The same letter had also been sent to the stock market regulator and to prominent newspapers. The letter, written by a person called Shankar Sharma, levelled several allegations against Tata Finance and its erstwhile managing director, Dilip Pendse. It charged that a prospectus issued by the company for a rights issue of preference shares contained falsified information. It also alleged that a fraud had been committed in the company.

At Bombay House, the headquarters of the Tata group, this unexpected letter marked the start of an unprecedented crisis. Ishaat Hussain, who was then the finance director of Tata Sons, described this situation a few years later in an article titled 'Grime and Salvation' published by Tata group publications: 'That letter alerted us, and further investigations revealed that there had indeed been some serious irregularities.' He went on to add, 'We were all taken aback.'

Tata Finance was a company with big ambitions. It had been established as the Tata group's flagship financial services firm. The company accepted fixed deposits from members of the public, and engaged in several areas of financing, including purchases of cars and consumer durables. It also had plans of entering merchant banking, securities trading and other financial advisory services. Heading the company was its managing director, Dilip Pendse, a high-profile man who was perceived as a financial whizz-kid. In addition, he was known to share a personal rapport with Ratan Tata.

The investigation ordered by the Tata group revealed that the company was in a major financial crisis. In fact, it was nearly insolvent. The reason was that the management of Tata Finance had lent approximately Rs 525 crore to some of its own subsidiary companies and affiliates, including a company called Nishkalp. A large part of that money had been invested in the stock market, in scrips of poor and speculative quality. Later investigations also revealed that many of these stock transactions were carried out to secure personal profits. When these scrips came crashing down, the original investments vanished and only a gaping black hole of more than Rs 500 crore remained, with nowhere to hide. The money that members of the public had entrusted Tata Finance with in the form of fixed deposits had vanished.

In this moment of crisis, Ratan Tata, as chairman of Tata Sons, led the way with thoughtful reflection and moral courage. Tata Sons could have merely adhered to its limited legal responsibilities. Instead, Ratan took the view that Tata Sons should do what is morally correct—it should protect the interests of every depositor, so that no one who had trusted the Tata name lost out on account of these ill-advised actions of the Tata Finance management.

R. Gopalakrishnan (Gopal), who was a director of Tata Sons and some other companies of the group at that time, narrated to me an interaction which happened at an annual general meeting of Tata Chemicals during the early days of this episode. Ratan Tata was present there, since he was also the chairman of this company.

Some elderly shareholders of Tata Chemicals, who had also deposited their money in Tata Finance, stood up and spoke with great emotion, bewailing the fact that they may lose their savings because of the fraud at Tata Finance. In fact, an elderly Parsi shareholder asked Ratan Tata, 'What will I do when my deposits are gone? What will I tell my wife when I return home tonight?'

Gopal says he was astonished when Ratan Tata stood up and boldly announced that Tata would stand behind every small depositor. Ratan went on to say that nobody needed to fear losing even a rupee of his or her savings. He made this commitment on the spot, and publicly. Gopal says, 'He [Ratan] instinctively acted on the principle that when there is a crisis, you just have to do what your sense of duty and conscience dictates.'

At his office in Bombay House, Ratan Tata took forward this commitment quickly. He recommended to the board of Tata Sons that they stand behind all the liabilities of Tata Finance, notwithstanding the fact that such a commitment was well beyond what the law of the land required. He backed this commitment by ensuring that Tata Sons and

Tata Industries quickly injected Rs 615 crore into Tata Finance both through cash and corporate guarantees.

On 25 July 2001, a public statement was issued, stating that Tata Finance was in distress because of a fraud that had been committed upon it, but that the Tata group would ensure no depositor lost his or her money. To ensure that depositors felt doubly safe, special counters were opened where depositors could withdraw their money. The clear instruction from Ratan Tata's office was that no depositor who wanted his money back should be turned away.

In fact, to ensure this across the country, Tata Finance also kept a helicopter on standby so that funds could be transported quickly by air if required. Fortunately, that helicopter was never used, because very few people actually withdrew their deposits. Such was their trust in the reassurance provided by Ratan Tata and the Tata group.

I must add a personal note here. I was a young manager in Tata Tea during those days, and I had invested in a fixed deposit of Rs 10,000 in Tata Finance. Not once did I even think of withdrawing this deposit, because Ratan Tata's statement removed any doubt from my mind.

I am sure that tens of thousands of other depositors felt similarly.

Reflecting on Ratan Tata's handling of the situation, Ishaat Hussain says, 'There is no parallel for this gesture in Indian corporate history.'

But this was not all. Ratan Tata also instructed Ishaat Hussain that 'there is to be no cover up, the guilty people must be punished'. Ishaat says that this was also quite unique, as many other corporates in India tend to sweep such incidents under the carpet so as to avoid public scrutiny. In addition, in this particular case, the managing director who had been accused, Dilip Pendse, was not just another senior executive of the Tata group. He was well known to Ratan Tata and a close colleague with whom he had worked for many years. But Ratan Tata decided to take this path because he had concluded that it was both legally and morally the correct thing to do.

Based on the results of its internal investigation, Tata Finance and Tata Industries filed a first information report (FIR) with the economic offences wing of the Mumbai Police against Dilip Pendse and certain other former Tata Finance employees. In 'Grime and Salvation', Ishaat Hussain says, 'We moved the courts when the Mumbai police filed a closure report with respect to our complaints. We took the stance that we will not let go of the culprits. We moved the Bombay High Court and got the investigation transferred to the Central Bureau of Investigation. In the Supreme Court too, our stand was vindicated. Six criminal complaints were filed in all, including three with the Delhi Police, and six complaints with SEBI for violation of various securities laws.'

Subsequently, Dilip Pendse was charge-sheeted in two complaints and taken into judicial custody. Ratan Tata's determination that the guilty should be given due punishment, regardless of how senior they were, had borne fruit.

This crisis in Tata Finance led to a lot of soul-searching at the headquarters of the Tata group. The systemic errors and failures which led to this episode were analysed in great detail, and many internal practices were tightened and changed to guard against the recurrence of such episodes. For readers who are interested in knowing more, I have recounted some of these changes in greater detail in my book *Tata Log*.

What stands out for me in this story is Ratan Tata's determination to do what he thought was morally correct.

In the midst of this unprecedented crisis, in the midst of adverse media reports and public reactions, he stood tall by every depositor, even if this far exceeded what was required in law. By pursuing the culprits, including the managing director, who was well known to him, he displayed an extraordinary level of transparency that is not seen often in the corporate world. He chose these actions because he thought they were the right thing to do.

Ishaat Hussain says, in his view, the Tata Finance episode impacted Ratan Tata deeply. In addition to bearing the weight of the entire episode and steering the group through this crisis, perhaps Ratan also felt a sense of betrayal. In fact, as Ishaat concluded this story, he told me with a sigh, 'It was a defining episode for Ratan. It weighed on him. He changed a lot after the crisis in Tata Finance.'

The Lake Natron Opportunity

During Ratan Tata's tenure as chairman of the Tata group, he also served as chairman of some of the larger Tata companies. One such company was Tata Chemicals, which was then in the business of branded salt, basic chemistry products and fertilizers. The Tatas had entered this business in the early 1940s, and the company had grown multifold thereafter. In keeping with its expertise in chemistry and the basic sciences, it pursued a goal of 'serving society through science'.

One of the key products in the company's portfolio was (and continues to be) soda ash, also known as sodium carbonate. This is an inorganic compound which is widely used across the world because it is required for the manufacture of commonly used products such as glass and detergents. Tata Chemicals is today the third-largest soda ash manufacturer globally, and scaling this business profitably has been a key business objective for the company over the past many decades.

In 2005, an exciting new opportunity around soda ash came to Ratan Tata and the board of Tata Chemicals. This was an opportunity to develop a large natural soda ash project on the edge of Lake Natron in the Rift Valley in Tanzania. The Government of Tanzania invited Tata Chemicals to explore this opportunity. The management and the board of directors of Tata Chemicals were enthused by this proposal because they felt it dovetailed very well with the company's growth ambitions, for multiple reasons.

First, soda ash was at the core of the company's business, hence the project was an excellent fit with its growth strategy. Second, this was a lucrative new business opportunity, which could potentially provide good economic returns. Third, this was an opportunity to mine naturally occurring soda ash, which was considered a more 'sustainable product' compared to synthetic soda ash. Finally, Tata Chemicals had already developed expertise on this front through a similar project in Kenya.

Under Ratan's chairmanship, the board of Tata Chemicals discussed this proposal at length, and was very supportive of taking it forward. In July 2005, the board provided its approval for progressing the project, including expenditure towards a feasibility study, appointment of consultants and other pre-project costs. It was also envisaged that a joint venture company would be formed, in which Tata Chemicals and the National Development Council (NDC) of Tanzania would be equal partners.

Work on the project began very enthusiastically. A senior team from Tata Chemicals visited Lake Natron. P.K. Ghose, who was the CFO of Tata Chemicals at that time, remembers his visit to the location. 'The whole place was very reddish, and looked very beautiful,' he recalls. Feasibility studies commenced in right earnest, and there was excitement in the air that the company would have yet another large growth engine soon, in the space of soda ash.

In essence, this project envisaged the mining of natural soda ash from Lake Natron. Let's visit this lake for a moment. It is a salt or alkaline lake located on Tanzania's border with Kenya, on a geological formation known as the East African Rift. The lake is fed primarily by a river and by mineral-rich hot springs. The unusual orange-red colour of the lake, as observed by P.K. Ghose, comes from the algae that flourish in its highly alkaline waters. Because of high levels of evaporation, the lake contains high concentrations of natron, or sodium carbonate decahydrate. In fact, this is the naturally occurring chemical which gives the lake its name.

This is also the chemical which gave rise to the business opportunity which was now being explored by the company. In simple terms, the proposed soda ash plant would pump the highly saline water from Lake Natron and then extract the sodium carbonate from this water, thus producing natural soda ash. Because of the high concentration of sodium carbonate in the lake, this was relatively easy and cost-effective to do, and therefore made for a very appealing business opportunity.

It was estimated that Lake Natron held a huge reserve of soda ash: around 4.7 billion cubic metres. The proposed plant would produce 5,00,000 tons of soda ash annually. Consultants appointed by Tata Chemicals drew up a detailed project report. In 2006, the board of directors approved a further tranche of expenditure towards various pre-project studies. By now, several crores of rupees had been committed to the project, which appeared to be progressing comfortably on track.

It was at this point that Ratan Tata received a message, reportedly from a well-known global personality, alerting him to something important. This message highlighted to Ratan that Lake Natron was the only regular breeding site for lesser flamingoes, a species of flamingoes that lives in Sub-Saharan Africa. A soda ash plant could threaten this breeding site, and that could in turn leave the lesser flamingoes of eastern Africa facing extinction. The message therefore urged Ratan to take this important factor into account before proceeding with the soda ash plant.

Other bodies such as the Royal Society for the Protection of Birds (RSPB) and Bird Life International had also begun raising this matter, and tabling strong concerns about the threat that a soda ash plant at Lake Natron could pose to the lesser flamingoes as well as to the ecosystem of the lake. It therefore became clear that there was an environmental angle that Tata Chemicals would have to take on board before finalizing this project.

Ratan Tata briefed the directors of Tata Chemicals about the message he had received. R. Gopalakrishnan, who served as vice chairman of the company at that time, recalls that this led to a lengthy and intense discussion amongst the directors. Ratan himself preferred to sit quietly during the initial part of this discussion after completing his briefing. He listened intently to what the other directors had to say.

There was no legal bar on progressing with the project—it had the support of the Government of Tanzania. In addition, it was economically lucrative, and would play an important role in the company's growth plans. Yet another point of view was that the company was too far down the road on this project, with the feasibility studies that had been carried out and the investments that had already been made. On the other hand, here was a very important environmental matter that had come up. Should the company undertake a project which ran the risk of endangering an entire species of birds, the lesser flamingoes?

Having heard all the directors, Ratan Tata is reported to have thanked them for all their inputs and then concluded saying that the company had to take this matter seriously. He advised the management to study the matter in detail and report back to the board.

R. Mukundan, who was a senior member of the Tata Chemicals leadership team at that time (he would later rise to become the managing director of the company), remembers Ratan Tata's advice to the management, 'Let us be science-led in our decision. Let us understand all the facts, and not be emotional.'

The facts soon became clear. A large majority of the world's population of lesser flamingoes live in East Africa, and Lake Natron is their primary breeding site. The natural soda ash project, as envisaged on the lakeside at that time, was likely to cause disruption at this breeding site. Flamingoes need a quiet and peaceful environment for nesting, and any disturbance could result in driving them away. Since this lake was the only regular breeding site for these lesser flamingoes, this could impact their reproduction and ultimately result in the extinction of this species. In addition, any such industrial project on the lakeside also posed a threat to the lake's fragile ecosystem.

The directors and the management discussed all these facts at length. Ratan Tata listened keenly once again as the conversation covered various scenarios and consequences. Eventually, as chairman of the company, Ratan presented his considered views. He is reported to have said that, on balance, having listened to all facts and all points of view, 'we should listen to our inner conscience. We should not cause damage to the environment for the sake of our business.'

Ratan knew that a decision not to take forward this project would cut off a potential growth engine for the business. In addition, it would also result in a significant financial write-off for the company, since a lot of pre-project expenses had already been incurred. Yet he came to this decision, not because it was required by any law, but because he thought it was the morally right thing to do.

In 2008, pursuant to these discussions, the company announced that it was putting the proposed plant on hold. R. Gopalakrishnan told media, 'The Tanzanian government invited us to come and prospect for soda ash in the Lake Natron valley. So the joint venture was formed to investigate the possibility of doing so.' He said that Tata Chemicals would wait for the Tanzanian government to work on the opposition raised by environmentalists and get clearance. 'Otherwise, we are not coming,' he added. By 2012, the company decided to exit the project.

P.K. Ghose recalls that Ratan Tata was never a man to accept a financial write-off easily. In fact, he would question every proposal put up to him for a write-off, asking management to consider all other alternatives. But in this case, P.K. Ghose remembers, Ratan accepted the write-off without demur, because of the strong moral context of the decision. The write-off was implemented in a single quarter, and this impacted the company's profitability materially during that period.

Ratan Tata led the decision not to take forward Tata Chemicals' participation in the Lake Natron project because he believed that an enterprise should put the larger good over narrow business objectives. The planet and the community were far more important than financial profits alone. For him, the right decision was to ensure that there was no risk to the survival of lesser flamingoes, notwithstanding the economic opportunity loss to the company.

The Missing Legal Clause

Bharat Vasani was, for many years, the chief legal officer and group general counsel at Tata Sons. In this expert role, he worked closely with Ratan Tata and the leadership team of the Tata group on many important legal matters. Bharat narrated this interesting story to me, of how Ratan Tata responded to a legal clause that went missing.

During Ratan Tata's tenure as chairman, the Tata group developed many successful partnerships with reputed global firms. One such business venture was under discussion with a well-known company. For the sake of this story, let me call this company ABC, because I am not in a position to reveal the real name here. Bharat Vasani was interacting with Ratan on various legal points relating to this venture.

After many rounds of discussions, a draft agreement was developed capturing all the key points of the partnership. After several iterations, most points on the agreement had been finalized. However, company ABC was insisting on one particular legal clause that Ratan Tata did not want included in the agreement. In fact, Ratan was quite uncomfortable with this clause.

The Tata group's disagreement with this specific clause was duly conveyed by Bharat to ABC. Tata Sons did not know how that company would respond. But it was known informally that the chairperson of ABC was quite clear about wanting this specific clause in the agreement.

When the final draft of the agreement came back from ABC to Tata Sons, there was a surprise in store. Bharat Vasani and his team found that this particular contentious clause was totally missing from the agreement. In other words, the agreement was now completely favourable to Tata Sons and everything was in readiness for the deal to be signed.

Bharat pointed this out to Ratan Tata, perhaps with some relief. However, Ratan had other thoughts on the matter. He turned to Bharat and said: 'This clause that we disagreed with is now missing. We should bring this to their (ABC's) attention and check with them. Have they accepted our suggestion to drop this clause, or is this an accidental omission?'

As Bharat listened, Ratan Tata continued on this point, to say: 'If they have knowingly agreed to drop this clause, then that is fine. But if this is accidental, then we should not take advantage of it.'

As advised by Ratan, Bharat duly pointed out the omission of the clause to ABC. Speaking to their general counsel, Bharat asked, 'Have you agreed to our request to delete this clause?'

The general counsel of that company was caught by surprise. 'Thank you for pointing this out,' she responded to Bharat, 'we never wanted to delete it. Omitting this clause was totally a mistake.'

So the contentious clause was reinstated and eventually it was part of the final agreement that was finally signed between Tata Sons and ABC.

Clearly, for Ratan Tata, the actual intent mattered more than the legal wording. If there had been an earlier divergence about some specific matter, he needed to know whether the other party had consciously taken this difference of view on board and decided to drop the matter. Going beyond the legal text to firmly ascertaining the other party's intentions, before signing off on the agreement, was essential. He was unwilling to take advantage of an inadvertent error by the other party, even if such an error favoured his own company. Because, in his view, this was the morally correct thing to do.

7

Fostering Fairness

Ratan Tata was not a man who thumped the table or raised his voice when he was unhappy. He was always soft-spoken, and even his mandates were conveyed softly and with utmost civility. Yet, people who knew him well could make out when he was upset from his body language and the sharp, steely look in his eyes.

Many people I interviewed for this book told me that the one thing that would upset him greatly was unfairness. If he felt that a decision was unfair to any set of stakeholders—employees, business partners, shareholders or the community at large—he would get visibly disturbed, and the anger would show on his face. Insisting on fairness and fostering it in all areas that he was responsible for was for him an integral part of doing the right thing.

Kishor Chaukar, who served as managing director of Tata Industries for many years, worked closely with Ratan Tata. He recalls a conversation with Ratan during the late 1990s, when he had just joined the Tata group. During this period, it had been decided to close down some Tata businesses. Ratan was very clear in how he wanted this process to be conducted, and he told Kishor, 'We must look after the staff and all other stakeholders. I do not want anybody to be harmed or treated unfairly.'

Ratan Tata believed that such fairness was a foundational principle on which the Tata group had been built, and hence it was particularly important that it was given the highest priority in every decision. Clearly, at least some part of this belief must have come from his close interactions with J.R.D. Tata, who strove to be scrupulously fair in everything that he did.

In a foreword that he wrote to a book titled *Code of Honour*, produced by Tata Group Publications in 2009, Ratan has written: 'We have to be fair to all our stakeholders. Being just to every constituent of the community is crucial. It is the cornerstone of the tremendous equity that Tata products and services enjoy, and the basis of the faith and trust reposed by people in Tata companies.'

Ratan was also acutely aware that India was a country that bore the burden of huge inequalities. He therefore felt that it was only fair and right that he and the Tata group do whatever they could to reduce these disparities. This came to the fore in many of his decisions, including the creation of several cancer hospitals in Assam and other states of north-east India, a region that is far less economically developed than other parts of the country.

It was therefore befitting that when the Assam government in 2025 chose a name for the upcoming electronics city that is poised to transform the industrial landscape of the state they named it the Ratan Tata Electronic City, to honour Ratan's contributions to Assam's industrial growth and economic development.

The stories in this chapter illustrate how fostering fairness was a driving force in Ratan Tata's life and career.

The IPO of Tata Consultancy Services

One of the more challenging decisions that Ratan Tata had to take during his stint as chairman of Tata Sons was the IPO of Tata Consultancy Services (TCS). TCS had begun its journey in 1968 as a computer division of Tata Sons, and it continued to be fully owned by Tata Sons for the next three decades. The company grew rapidly and spread its wings around the world even as it progressed impressively on its journey of becoming a global IT services powerhouse.

By the 1990s, TCS had become one of the top performing companies of the Tata group, and by then, private estimates put the valuation of the company at close to Rs 1 lakh crore, a very impressive figure, virtually unheard of in those days. The question that came up in the late 1990s was: Would Tata Sons list TCS on the stock exchange? Despite many views to the contrary, Ratan Tata decided to go ahead with the listing for a few key reasons, one of the most important being that the listing would permit TCS to reward its employees with stock options. The listing would also bring in a large tranche of funds that Tata Sons could use for the modernization of other major Tata companies.

Ishaat Hussain worked closely with Ratan Tata and Noshir Soonawala (the then vice chairman of Tata Sons, and a close confidant of Ratan) on this listing. It was decided that Tata Sons would offer around 14 per cent of TCS's equity shares to the public, and that these shares would be listed on the National Stock Exchange (NSE) and the Bombay Stock Exchange (BSE). In 2004, Tata Sons moved forward with this IPO. It was a huge offering, and the single-largest IPO by a private sector Indian company until then. There were many complexities inherent in such an offering, and Ishaat says that Ratan Tata had to evaluate innumerable options before coming to the right structure of the IPO.

The IPO opened on 29 July 2004—the hundredth birth anniversary of J.R.D. Tata, who had co-founded TCS. It closed a week later, on 5 August 2004. Ishaat Hussain recalls a hectic week of roadshows marketing TCS to the investing public. Eventually, Ratan Tata and he met with bankers at the Chambers in the Taj Mahal Hotel, Mumbai, to decide on two of the most important elements of an IPO: the allocation and the pricing of shares.

The public issue had been oversubscribed several times. Specifically, the interest from small retail investors had been spectacular. In fact, the issue was oversubscribed by these small retail investors alone. This was amazing, given that the size of the issue exceeded $1 billion, and let us remember that this was way back in 2004.

However, when the matter of allocation of shares came up, it was highlighted to Ratan Tata that as per the rules which were then in place, around 65 per cent of all shares had to be allocated to institutional investors (also termed qualified institutional bidders) and non-institutional investors (high-net-worth individuals). This meant that the quota for small retail investors was restricted to less than 40 per cent of the total. Therefore, these small retail investors would only get a fraction of the shares high-net-worth they had applied for, whereas the big institutional investors would get their full allocations, and in much larger quantities.

When Ratan Tata heard about this, he became visibly upset. He said that this was very unfair to the small investor. In fact, he wanted as many shares of TCS as possible to be owned by the common man, not by elite wealthy investors or by institutions alone. Ishaat Hussain recalls that Ratan said that he was ashamed that he had to be party to the proposed allotment pattern which was blatantly unfair. In addition, Ratan Tata also voiced his concern to SEBI, and advised Ishaat Hussain to take up the matter at the right fora.

Ishaat was then a member of the primary markets committee of SEBI, where he duly took up this matter. However, investment bankers put up their own arguments for why the high institutional quota was required.

Eventually, the allotment quotas remained unchanged for the TCS public issue, much to Ratan Tata's intense dissatisfaction.

The matter of pricing the shares now came up for discussion. The public issue had gone through the book-building process, within a range of Rs 750 to Rs 900. Typically, the final pricing is decided based on how the book has been built. Given that the issue had been oversubscribed, and many investors had bid at the top, Ishaat Hussain recommended that the issue be priced at Rs 900, which was the top end of the range. 'I was doing my job as the CFO of Tata Sons,' Ishaat recalls, 'and my job was to maximize value for Tata Sons.'

Ratan Tata, however, disagreed with his CFO's advice. He thought that the fair thing to do would be to price the issue at much less than Rs 900, thus providing a benefit for shareholders, and in particular for small retail investors. He turned to Ishaat and told him, 'Let us leave something on the table for the investors. Let us not try to maximize value only for ourselves.'

Based on Ratan's advice, the issue was priced at Rs 850 per share, which was somewhere in the middle of the range. As a result, Tata Sons had to forgo some part of the amount that it could have raised from the offer had they decided to price it at the top end. Ishaat says that this was Ratan Tata's way of being fair to all the major stakeholders in the offer, rather than trying to extract the highest value for only the seller.

'Ratan Tata's desire to be fair in all his dealings was a very strong urge in him,' Ishaat concludes. He recalls Ratan telling him, 'We must not only be seen to be doing the right thing, but we must be actually doing the right thing.' The TCS IPO is a very good instance of this principle in action.

Where Shall We Make the Nano?

One of the most path-breaking products ever to come out of independent India was the small car, Tata Nano. This was a project close to Ratan Tata's heart. It came out of his desire to create an affordable car for middle-class Indians, a car that would enable them to easily upgrade from scooters. Ratan had observed that scooters often carried an entire Indian family—the husband in the driver's seat, the wife sitting behind him, holding a baby, and an elder child standing in front of the husband—which was unsafe. He felt that one good way of resolving this issue and providing safe family transportation was to create a small car that was affordably priced.

Ratan Tata first began speaking about such a vehicle in 2000, soon after the successful launch of the Tata Indica, the first indigenous Indian car. The success of the Tata Indica had given a huge boost to the confidence of the Tata Motors team and to Ratan's own confidence, and he was soon thinking about the next game changer: an affordable car. These preliminary thoughts took some time to mature, but by 2003, a young project team was in place. Leading the team was one of the finest engineers in Tata Motors, Girish Wagh.

At the Geneva Motor Show in 2003, Ratan Tata was interviewed by the *Financial Times*. He spoke at this interview about the small car, and when asked about its likely cost, he replied that it could be around $2500 (the equivalent of Rs 1 lakh at that time's foreign exchange conversion rate). The *Financial Times* ran a story based on this interview. In actual fact, the price of the car had not been firmed up at that stage. However, rather than issue a rebuttal, Ratan chose to take this figure as a target. The Nano was thereafter widely referred to as 'Tata's Rs 1 lakh car'.

Even as the design and engineering processes of the car made good progress, one of the decisions that Ratan Tata and his team had to take was deciding the location for the factory that would manufacture it. In 2005, this exercise began in right earnest.

An ideal location would have been somewhere in the vicinity of Pune, where Tata Motors had its main car facility. This is where the Tata Indica was being manufactured and assembled, and also where a lot of Tata Motors' engineering talent was housed. In addition, Tata Motors had already developed an automobile component suppliers' ecosystem in this western region of India.

Yet another 'automobile cluster' was near Chennai in Tamil Nadu. Hyundai had established its car factory in Sriperumbudur in this zone, and Tamil Nadu also offered good infrastructure and roads. An auto ecosystem existed here too.

A third region that could have been considered was the National Capital Region (NCR), which was one of the most developed regions in the country, and where Maruti Suzuki, the market leader in cars, had built a good ecosystem, including availability of talent and a good supplier base.

Two other states that came up for discussion were Karnataka and Uttaranchal, particularly since Tata Motors already had manufacturing plants at Dharwad and Pant Nagar respectively, in these two states.

Ravi Kant, who was the managing director of Tata Motors at that time, and Girish Wagh, the young project leader of the Nano project, both vividly remember these interactions with Ratan Tata. Girish recalls visiting Tamil Nadu, Punjab and parts of Maharashtra to assess sites. It was at that point that Ratan Tata turned to the team and told them, 'Please evaluate West Bengal as well.'

Girish recalls that his colleagues and he were surprised because West Bengal had a communist state government at that time and was not perceived as friendly towards industry.

Ratan Tata must have understood the unease in his team, so he explained to them that he had had more than one conversation with Buddhadeb Bhattacharjee, the then chief minister of West Bengal. Buddhadeb was very progressive in his thinking, and was committed to the industrial development of the state. If the Tatas were to set up a large unit in West Bengal, other industrial groups were also likely to follow, leading to the future economic growth of a state which was trailing behind in industrial development.

Ratan Tata then looked around at the team and told them the real reason why he was recommending West Bengal: 'We owe it to our nation that we participate in the re-industrialization of eastern India.'

Clearly, in Ratan's mind, there was a need for the Tatas, as the country's largest business group, to foster fairness by promoting equitable industrial development across the country. Having already established new plants in the recent past in Pune in Maharashtra, Dharwad in Karnataka and Pant Nagar in Uttaranchal, he perhaps felt that Tata Motors should now consider eastern India and West Bengal, which lag behind the rest of the country on many metrics of industrial development.

This direction from Ratan led the team to examine three alternative sites in West Bengal, eventually culminating in the selection of a place named Singur. This small town provided excellent connectivity by road, was only around 40 kilometres away from Kolkata and not too far away from the Kolkata airport. In addition, West Bengal was also willing to offer an excellent incentive package to the Tata group to attract investment to the state.

As I reflect on this choice of Singur, what strikes me is that this was not the easy route to take, by any stretch of economic or operational logic. Going to industrialized regions such as Tamil Nadu, Maharashtra, the NCR or Karnataka would have been easier for Tata Motors—with their established infrastructure, vendor ecosystem and auto industry–trained talent. Yet, Ratan chose West Bengal and Singur because he thought that this was the fair and right thing to do, that it would help in some small way to reduce the economic disparities that existed between different regions of the country.

The announcement of Singur as the site for the Tata Nano was made during May 2006. Within around six months thereafter, Tata Motors was given possession of the land on which the factory and its allied facilities would come up. Girish Wagh recalls that while his team and he had initial misgivings about West Bengal and Singur because of the state's patchy history of industrialization and industrial harmony, the entire team now got down to work with a very positive frame of mind. They were also confident that suppliers and others would follow them to Singur with ancillary units because of Tata Motors' deep relationships with their business partners.

Unfortunately, however, matters did not progress smoothly in Singur. As soon as the project was announced, agitations began at Singur, against the state government's proposal to acquire nearly 1000 acres of farmland for this project. Land acquisition was being handled by the government, and Tata Motors had no role to play in this process. After the land lease deal was finalized, the agitation grew in intensity. The agitation was led by the feisty Mamta Banerjee, leader of the Trinamool Congress party, which was at that time in the opposition in West Bengal. What was initially a sporadic protest by a few local villagers soon snowballed into a huge political issue.

Tata Motors had, in the meantime, begun work at the site. Construction of the factory facilities began in early 2007, and a large team from Tata Motors was based out of Singur. Significant investment was made in building the plant, including important facilities such as the engine manufacturing machinery, the paint shop, the assembly lines and all related utility infrastructure. A beautifully written book which has detailed the Nano venture (*Small Wonder: The Making of the Nano*, authored by Philip Chacko, Christabelle Noronha and Sujata Agrawal) has mentioned that during the first eighteen months, around Rs 1500 crore of expenditure had already been incurred by Tata Motors. A vendor park also came up at Singur to house the facilities of parts suppliers, and these suppliers had made investments too. By now, around 2000 people were based at the site.

But as the agitation intensified, Girish Wagh got increasingly concerned. There were many instances where workers were intimidated by the agitators. A writ petition was filed in the Kolkata High Court, challenging the acquisition of land on the basis that it would ruin the livelihoods of thousands of farmers. In August 2008, Mamta Banerjee launched an indefinite dharna outside the Nano plant, demanding that 400 acres of land be given back to the farmers. For some time, employees were forced to stay within the plant until the police arrived. By now, Girish was beginning to think about an alternative to Singur, though he hoped against hope that the Nano would still stay there.

Girish Wagh recalls a meeting with Ratan Tata during this period. On Independence Day (15 August) 2008, Ratan Tata was in Pune, and he asked to meet Girish to get a complete report on Singur. After Girish briefed him, Ratan appreciated the work done by the team and the suppliers, and specifically mentioned that all these efforts would contribute to the re-industrialization of West Bengal. However, he also told Wagh that employee safety was of the highest importance, and this would be a key factor in taking any decision regarding Singur.

Ravi Kant remembers this time vividly too. He recalls that the Tata Motors team had put their heart and soul into making the Nano plant at Singur happen. However, as the agitation intensified, he remembers speaking to Ratan Tata and telling him, 'We have built a plant in Singur. But I am not sure if we can run a plant there.' He said this primarily because of factors relating to the safety of people.

As a result of the worsening situation, Ratan Tata approved the suspension of work at the Singur plant on 23 August 2008. Even at that stage, Ratan was not entirely sure that he would pull the plant out of Singur. A lot of capital had been invested there already, the plant was virtually at the state of pre-commissioning, and he still hoped that the chief minister, whom he held in high esteem, could find a solution to the issue. However, in his mind, the most important thing now was the safety of the employees of Tata Motors, the company's suppliers and everyone posted at Singur.

Ratan Tata sought a meeting with the chief minister. On 3 October 2008, he flew to Kolkata for this meeting. He was accompanied by Ravi Kant, who recalls that even during the flight, Ratan had not made up his mind completely about shifting the plant out of Singur. However, during the one-and-a-half-hour-long meeting, he reached a final conclusion. He told the chief minister that the team from Tata Motors could not work at Singur under such intimidating circumstances, and hence they would have to move the Nano plant away from the state.

Ravi Kant recalls, 'This was a very bold decision that put the interests of our people first, despite all the work already completed, all the investments that had already been done. It would also result in a considerable delay of the project. I cannot think of anyone else who could have taken such a decision.'

Clearly, Ratan Tata had decided that this was the right thing to do, that remaining in Singur would be totally unfair and also potentially dangerous to employees and their families. The safety of the people was far more important than other factors.

Later that day, Ratan Tata addressed a press conference at the Taj Bengal Hotel in Kolkata. Girish Wagh recalls the clarity and determination with which Ratan spoke to the media. Ratan said, 'By taking all things into account, mainly the well-being of our employees, the safety of our contractors and vendors also, we have taken the very regretful decision to move the Nano project out of West Bengal.'

The Nano plant was thereafter shifted out from Singur to Sanand in Gujarat, at the invitation of Narendra Modi, the then chief minister of Gujarat. That is another story altogether.

Girish Wagh says that this story of Nano and Singur threw up a very important aspect of Ratan Tata's personality—his determination to do the fair and right thing, always. To begin with, Ratan was driven by a sense of fairness in nation-building in choosing Singur. He wanted to help in the economic development of eastern India, a region that was lagging behind the rest of the country. However, when the agitation at Singur intensified, he concluded that the only correct and fair decision would be to protect the safety of employees and associates, and he acted on this priority, overriding all other considerations.

The Sale of Hitech Drilling

In 1985, the Tata group entered the business of drilling and related services for the exploration of oil and other hydrocarbon resources. The name of the company established to take forward this venture was Hitech Drilling Services India Limited. Hitech Drilling was promoted by Tata Industries Limited, a company which was led at that time by Ratan Tata. Tata Industries spearheaded the Tata group's entry into many new fields of technology.

For the first few years, Hitech Drilling was a joint venture between Tata Industries and a subsidiary of Schlumberger Inc. However, when the initial technology tie-up ended, Schlumberger Inc. exited the company and Tata Industries continued as the promoter. The company was converted into a public limited firm and was listed on the Indian stock exchange.

By the late 1990s, as an integral part of corporate restructuring efforts, the Tata group was considering exiting the oil drilling business. The board of Tata Industries, chaired by Ratan Tata, had agreed on this strategic direction. Following this board mandate, Kishor Chaukar, the managing director of Tata Industries, had commenced a search for potential buyers of Hitech Drilling. Tata Industries held a 22.5 per cent equity stake in this company, and the objective was to ensure an exit at the best possible valuation.

Kishor Chaukar, who worked for many years with Ratan Tata as a key member of his leadership team, recalls taking forward this process in close consultation with Ratan. Eventually, there were some fruitful discussions with a company called Aban Loyd Chiles Offshore, which was a prominent offshore drilling services provider. Aban Loyd had been founded in 1986 by M.A. Abraham, and it was now keen to acquire Hitech Drilling, which would help take the company to a market leadership position in the Indian offshore drilling industry.

Chaukar and Abraham began negotiating this acquisition, and an agreement was finally reached by which Aban Loyd would buy the Tata Industries' 22.5 per cent equity stake in Hitech Drilling at a price well ahead of Rs 100 per share. This price was also far higher than the prevailing market price of the share at that time, reflecting factors such as the control premium that Aban Loyd was willing to pay for the large chunk of shares. This in-principle agreement was subject to clearance by Ratan Tata and thereafter formal consideration by the boards of both companies.

As per the SEBI takeover and acquisition rules prevailing at that time, Aban would also have to buy at least 20 per cent of the equity held by the public at the same price. In other words, Aban would have to buy the 22.5 per cent equity stake from Tata Industries as well as an additional 20 per cent equity from public shareholders at this same price.

Kishor Chaukar requested a meeting with Ratan Tata to inform him about this in-principle agreement. He was hoping that Ratan would be happy and approve the proposal, but Ratan turned around and told him, 'Kishore, I would like to know some more details about this.'

Ratan then asked him, 'Are we selling our entire holding in the company?' Kishore responded that this was indeed the case, that Tata Industries would exit Hitech Drilling by selling its entire 22.5 per cent holding at the price which had been agreed upon.

Ratan wanted to know, 'What happens to the public shareholders of Hitech Drilling in this deal?'

Chaukar explained to Ratan that, as per SEBI rules, Aban Loyd would have to buy an additional 20 per cent of equity from the public at the same price.

Ratan listened to him, thought about this for a minute and then asked him, 'What about the rest of the equity shares held by the public, including by small shareholders? What happens to them?'

Chaukar explained to him that they would have to take their chances with the new promoter, Aban Loyd, which was buying the company from Tata Industries.

Ratan Tata then asked Chaukar for his own assessment of what would happen to the market price of shares when the Tata group exited the company. Chaukar explained to him that the price could potentially move either way based on a number of factors, but there was a possibility of prices falling as investor sentiment could be driven by the exit of the Tata group.

When he heard this, Ratan turned to Kishor and told him, 'Kishor, I feel that this is unfair to all the small shareholders who have invested in Hitech Drilling because of the Tata name. I feel very uncomfortable with this proposal.'

He then asked Chaukar, 'Is there any way that Aban Loyd can buy 100 per cent of the equity of the company? Can they buy all the shares held by all shareholders at the same price, so that every shareholder gets the same price as we do? That would be fair.'

Chaukar explained that this could happen. However, the buyer would, in all likelihood, pay a lower amount per share, because he was now buying 100 per cent of the equity, and therefore would have to take into account factors such as the overall valuation of the company. The buyer would also have to invest a far greater amount of cash for the purchase. As a result, Tata Industries would obtain a lower overall amount for its own 22.5 per cent equity stake.

Ratan Tata asked Chaukar for his assessment of the difference in overall value that Tata Industries would obtain should this route be taken. Chaukar produced the details, and Ratan Tata then told him firmly and clearly, 'We should take this financial hit, and we should request Aban Loyd to buy out 100 per cent of the equity. I feel this would be the fair way.'

Clearly, Ratan Tata had come to the conclusion that fairness to all shareholders was more important than maximizing the amount that the Tata group would earn from this sale.

After some further discussion, Aban Loyd agreed to buy 100 per cent of the equity of Hitech Drilling, including all the equity shares held by small shareholders. However, as Kishor Chaukar had rightly forecast, they now offered a lower price of Rs 92 per share. An announcement on this subject, published in national newspapers, read: 'Tata Industries has, in the largest ever merger and acquisition in the Indian offshore drilling industry, sold its 22.5 per cent stake in Hitech Drilling to Aban Loyd Chiles Offshore, at Rs 92 per share.

'Aban Loyd Chiles will subsequently make an open offer for the entire outstanding equity at the same price, taking its total acquisition cost to Rs 1.87 billion. The price of transaction represents a[n] 81 per cent premium to the current market price of the scrip.'

Ratan Tata had done what he thought was the right thing to do, even if it meant a lower financial outcome to the Tatas. No wonder hundreds of millions of Indians reposed such trust in him, because trust and fairness go hand in hand.

8

Care and Compassion

In January 2021, a news report about Ratan Tata suddenly went viral. The report had nothing to do with the Tata group's businesses, or even Tata Trusts. It merely said that Ratan Tata had travelled all the way from his home in Mumbai to the Friends Society in Pune to spend some time with a former employee who had been unwell for two years.

This was a private visit, and would have gone completely unnoticed, except for a post on LinkedIn written by a person named Yogesh Desai who got to know about the visit. Yogesh also posted a picture of Ratan wearing a mask (since this was during the pandemic) and standing in the parking lot of the housing society.

Yogesh Desai's post said, 'This is how legends are made. No media, no bouncers, only commitment towards loyal employees. There is a lot to learn for all entrepreneurs and businessmen that money is not everything. All that matters is being a great human being. Hats off, Sir!! I bow my head in respect.'

Ratan Tata's visit to that ailing employee in Pune highlights one of the defining characteristics of the man: his care for the people who worked with him, and also for needy people whom he may not have known well. His compassion went beyond human beings—his love and care for stray dogs and animals is legendary. In fact, he was the driving force behind the creation of the Small Animal Hospital by Tata Trusts, a veterinary referral centre with specialists and cutting-edge facilities exclusively dedicated to dogs and cats.

For Ratan Tata, care and compassion were always the right way to go. Where did this instinct come from? I have never had the opportunity to discuss this with him, so I can only surmise. Perhaps one key source was his grandmother, Lady Navajbai Tata, a most generous and caring soul. She donated to charitable causes grand houses that she had inherited from her husband, Sir Ratanji Tata. Way back in 1926, she also established an institute in Mumbai to provide a source of livelihood to needy women of the Parsi community. As a young boy, Ratan lived with her for many years and would have seen her in action.

Yet another source could well have been Ratan's early professional years at Tata Steel in Jamshedpur. There, he would have seen the extensive community outreach work that Tata Steel had done over the decades in taking care of needy and underprivileged people, including providing them extensive medical and related facilities.

He would also have been influenced by stories of the founder of the Tata group, Jamsetji Tata, including how Jamsetji, more than a century earlier, introduced pioneering welfare measures such as accident insurance, pension fund, provident fund, medical and educational facilities to take care of the employees of his first greenfield industry, Empress Mills at Nagpur.

Perhaps a future biographer will examine these sources and their impacts with greater clarity. Suffice it to say here that care and compassion was an integral part of who Ratan Tata was. This was perhaps best articulated by Noel Tata, who succeeded Ratan Tata as chairman of Tata Trusts, in an excellent speech about Ratan that he delivered at an ET (*Economic Times*) awards event in March 2025—'In his individual capacity as well he (Ratan Tata) was forever willing to lend a helping hand to people and causes. Empathy came naturally to him and this was evident to the many whose lives he touched.'

I have experienced this myself on more than one occasion during my career of over thirty-five years with the Tata group. For instance, when my father passed away in February 2006, one of the first messages I received was a personal letter of condolence from Ratan Tata. I do not know how he got to hear about my father's demise, but the fact that he sent me this warm personal letter amidst all his responsibilities as chairman of the Tata group once again demonstrated to me that he sincerely cared for the people who worked with him.

The real-life incidents narrated below also bring out one of the most endearing facets of Ratan Tata's personality. Business leaders are generally known to be tough and demanding people, and it is rare to come across a leader like Ratan, who was also caring and compassionate at the same time.

Love and Care for Dogs and Animals

Ratan Tata loved dogs, animals and birds. In the midst of all his numerous official responsibilities, he prioritized their well-being because he thought it was the right thing to do to speak up for and help animals, who have no voice to champion their own.

Bombay House, the headquarters of the Tata group, is unique in being a home for stray dogs. Ever since I joined the Tata group in 1987, I have always seen stray dogs in the foyer of the premises. Ratan Tata loved these dogs. There are pictures I have seen of Ratan sitting down on the steps of Bombay House, playing with them.

When Ratan entered Bombay House each morning, he would pass by these dogs on his way up to his office which was located on the fourth floor. He would observe them as he went by. On one particular day, as he walked past the foyer, he felt that one of the dogs was not looking too well.

As soon as he went up to his office, he advised his assistant: 'Can you have a veterinary doctor look at this dog? He does not seem well at all.' The fact that he did this immediately, in the midst of hundreds of other official things that must have been on his mind, indicates the genuine care that he had for these animals.

A person who has worked closely with Ratan Tata narrated to me another story that brought alive the same care and compassion for living beings. Just outside Ratan

Tata's corner office on the fourth floor of Bombay House was a small terrace garden, full of green shrubs and plants. It is a lovely patch of greenery that overlooks the busy Fort area of Mumbai. Once, when Ratan stepped out on this balcony, perhaps to take in a breath of fresh air, he found a little bird which had fallen there. Stopping all other work, he called his assistant and said, 'Can we please call a vet who can help treat this little bird?' His office then kept apart other work for some time, and immediately got in touch with an expert, Pradeep D'Souza, also known as the 'birdman of Mumbai', to help treat this injured bird.

Ratan Tata's keenness to provide a safe space for stray dogs has been highlighted in a beautiful story narrated on the social media platform LinkedIn by N. Chandrasekaran (Chandra), chairman of Tata Sons. Sometime in 2017, after becoming chairman, Chandra expressed a desire to renovate Bombay House. This building had not been touched ever since its opening in 1924, nearly a century ago. Many people cautioned Chandra that Ratan Tata may not like such a renovation, particularly because Bombay House is regarded as a revered temple by everyone in the Tata group.

When Chandra finally mentioned the renovation, Ratan had one important question for him. 'Where will the dogs go?' He was referring to the stray dogs at the reception of Bombay House.

Chandra then told Ratan Tata that the plan was to build a kennel for these dogs in the renovated headquarters. When Bombay House was reopened after the renovation in 2018, Ratan Tata wanted to first see the kennel. He went there and was happy to see its thoughtful design, which reflected how well the dogs would be cared for.

Ratan Tata's question to Chandra—'Where will the dogs go?'—was not just about the dogs. It was a reflection of how important the values of care and compassion were in Ratan's life in his quest to do what he thought was right.

Yet another story about Ratan Tata prioritizing care and compassion over everything else was narrated to me by Suhel Seth, well-known businessman, columnist and speaker. In February 2018, Ratan Tata was scheduled to receive a lifetime achievement award for his philanthropic efforts from Prince Charles (now King Charles III) at Buckingham Palace in London. This event had been organized by the British Asian Trust, and Suhel Seth had been in touch with Ratan in this regard.

The event was slated for 6 February. Suhel had reached London two or three days ahead of the date of the function. As soon as he landed in London, he saw several missed calls on his cellphone from Ratan Tata.

So he called back and asked, 'Mr Tata, what has happened?'

Ratan Tata told Suhel that one of his dogs had fallen terribly ill. Ratan had two pet dogs, Tango and Tito, and one of them was unwell. Ratan said, 'I cannot leave him and come to London.'

Suhel tried reasoning with Mr Tata that this was a very prestigious event, with Prince Charles himself attending. However, Ratan Tata refused to budge, and he did not come to London. He preferred to stay behind at home in Mumbai to look after his sick pet dog, even if it meant missing out on such a coveted event. For Ratan, this was clearly the right thing to do.

Suhel Seth then had the task of conveying to Prince Charles that Ratan Tata was unable to attend the awards event because of his pet dog's illness. Suhel says that Prince Charles listened to him and replied, 'That's a man. That's the man that Ratan is. That is why the house of Tata is what it is. That is why it is on a stable course.'

How can I conclude this section without speaking about Goa, one of Ratan Tata's favourite dogs? Goa was so named because his origins were from Goa. As a small stray puppy, he had jumped into the car of a visiting senior Tata officer, Freddy Talati, who had brought him from Goa all the way to Bombay House.

Goa had a very special relationship with Ratan Tata. After Ratan had retired as chairman of Tata Sons, he had moved his office from Bombay House to the third floor of a nearby heritage building, Elphinstone House, which was located near Horniman Circle in the Fort area of Mumbai. Goa would walk across to Elphinstone House, get into the lift, go up to the third floor and walk into Ratan Tata's office all by himself. He would sit next to Ratan Tata on the sofa in his office. Ratan would pet him there, and ensure that he was well taken care of. In fact, Ratan Tata actually had a small bed created for Goa in the conference room, to ensure that the dog slept comfortably while he was visiting. Their relationship symbolized the immense love and care that can exist between man and dog.

Apart from the personal care that he displayed towards dogs and other animals, Ratan Tata was keen to create institutional facilities for the proper care of animals. One such dream came true towards the end of his life, when Tata Trusts' Small Animal Hospital officially opened its doors in Mumbai on 1 July 2024. The hospital is a 200-bed facility that offers advanced medical care for small animals like dogs and cats, including emergency care, CT scans, MRI, X-rays, ultrasound and specialized surgery units. It also has a dedicated facility for stray animal welfare.

Ratan had personally championed the project, and this hospital was perhaps his final gift to the nation while he was still alive. It continues to remind us of his care and compassion.

The Heroes of the Taj

On 26 November 2008, the city of Mumbai was attacked by armed terrorists who had crossed the seas from Pakistan to India. It was a dastardly attack, which spanned several locations in Mumbai. As many as 166 people were killed and over 300 were injured. This was one of the darkest hours ever in the history of India's financial capital.

One of the locations that was attacked that day was the Taj Mahal Palace Hotel, located just across the Gateway of India in South Mumbai. This iconic luxury hotel had been constructed by Jamsetji Tata, founder of the Tata group, more than a century earlier, in 1903. He had built the hotel as a grand symbol for Mumbai in the aftermath of the bubonic plague that had ravaged the city during the 1890s. Thereafter, the Taj had always been an integral part of Mumbai's skyline, and it also represented the best in Indian hospitality.

At around 9.30 p.m. on the night of 26 November, four armed terrorists entered the Taj and began wantonly shooting people within the hotel. This was a cowardly, ferocious attack on unarmed guests and staff. The terrorists wandered around the corridors of the hotel, using their weapons to kill mercilessly.

Ratan Tata had returned home that night after a full day's work. Soon thereafter, he received news of the attack. The operators at the hotel switchboard had been informed by people at the reception about the terrorists, and they had in turn conveyed this information to senior Tata officers.

Ratan Tata received calls from two of his senior colleagues, informing him of what was happening at the Taj. One of these calls was from R.K. Krishna Kumar (KK), director of Tata Sons and vice chairman of the Indian Hotels Company, which owns the Taj Hotel—a person we will meet at various points in this story, since he played a key role in it. Soon thereafter, Ratan left his home in Colaba and reached the Taj by around 10.30 p.m. By then, the police had also arrived, and a large posse of policemen was standing in the foyer area. KK had also reached there, along with his wife Ratna.

In that charged moment, Ratan attempted to push his way through and enter the hotel without considering the consequences of his action. The police rightly prevented him from getting to the door. KK also tried to enter the hotel, but a driver called Kamlesh fell at his feet and dragged him away. Immediately thereafter, they were led away by the police to a place of safety.

So Ratan now stood on the pavement outside the Taj, accompanied by KK and Ratna, looking in despair and disbelief at their beloved hotel, now under attack. He walked up and down the pavement, unable to digest the reality of what was going on. He was aghast and deeply saddened as he watched flames leap out of the Taj. He could hear a number of gunshots and explosions from inside the hotel. The fact that there were hundreds of guests and staff members inside who could be attacked and killed by the terrorists at any time caused him extreme anxiety.

Ratan stayed there for many hours that night, and the next morning he was back again.

H.N. Shrinivas (Shrinivas), who was at that time the chief human resources officer of the Taj group of hotels, has described vividly to me how Ratan Tata stood on the pavement with other senior executives of the Taj as a mark of solidarity with the people within the hotel. KK has written about how Ratan was outside the Taj for about three days, 'sharing the agony, helpless yet determined to endure and to extend a helping hand'. A few years later, KK reflected on some of these moments in a personal conversation with me at his office. As he spoke, I could feel the intense emotions of that night still deeply embedded in his mind.

Meanwhile, within the hotel, the four terrorists were unleashing waves of terror and death. However, the staff of the Taj stood by the guests and went well beyond the call of duty to protect them. Indeed, the staff were the heroes of the entire episode as they refused to run away. Instead, with their excellent knowledge of the hotel, and with extraordinary presence of mind, they quickly implemented many ideas to protect the guests.

Here is one example of this. All the kitchen staff, from chefs to trainees, came together to link arms with each other and form a human chain that provided a safe and clear path for guests to reach one of the back exits of the hotel through the kitchen corridors. Many guests were able to exit safely. But soon the terrorists appeared there and started firing. The staff pushed guests who were still in the corridor into an area of the hotel called 'The Chambers', firmly closed the door and shut off all the lights. By doing all this, they saved the lives of around 200 guests.

However, in the process of protecting guests, many chefs and kitchen staff tragically lost their lives. Chef Vijay Banga, assistant chef Kaizan Kamdin, assistant chef Zaheen Mateen, management trainee Boris Rego, assistant chef Hemant Taleem, senior steward Thomas Varghese and steward Faustine Martis were some of the Taj staff whose lives were so sadly cut short. Their extraordinary courage and selflessness was a display of the values that they lived for every day—the values of putting their guests first and foremost, of going beyond the call of duty whenever required. Their names are etched in history forever.

In the early hours of 27 November, some hours after the terrorists had struck the Taj, elite commandos of the National Security Guard and marine commandos of the Indian Navy entered the hotel. They helped evacuate the guests and staff safely and launched a hunt for the terrorists. By the third day of the attack, all four terrorists had been flushed out and killed by these commandos.

After this had been accomplished, on the morning of 29 November, Ratan Tata and KK were finally permitted by the commandos to enter the Taj. By then, Ratan had stood in vigil for almost two and a half days—nearly sixty hours—on the pavement outside, except for brief breaks to go home or to his office. He was there until every guest had been evacuated safely, and his presence was a source of great motivation to the entire team.

Now, as he entered the Taj, he saw scenes of destruction all around. Shrinivas, who was there, recalls, 'It was looking like a battlefield, completely ransacked. Chandeliers, paintings, wall hangings ... everything was broken and in pieces. Ratan Tata had tears in his eyes, but he also had steely determination on his face. At some point that day, he sat on a torn sofa and engaged us in a discussion.'

What became clear during this discussion was the firm resolve to restore the Taj back to its glory as quickly as possible. In fact, the first official statement from the Taj, which had been released on the morning of 27 November, reflected Ratan's resolve: 'We cannot replace the lives that have been lost, and we will never forget the terrifying events of last night, but we must stand together, shoulder to shoulder as citizens of India, and rebuild what has been destroyed. We must show that we cannot be disabled or destroyed, but that such a heinous act will only make us stronger.'

It was decided that the Taj would open again for business within a month—a very short timeline given the amount of destruction. Indeed, in less than three weeks from then, the Taj reopened for business on 21 December 2008, with all rooms of the tower wing ready for guests. Speaking on this occasion from the front porch of the Taj, Ratan Tata paid tribute to the people who had lost their lives and to the injured, to the unprecedented spirit displayed by the staff and then he said, 'We can be hurt, but we cannot be knocked down. The Taj will stand for another hundred years and will stand as a tribute to the tenacity of our people.'

There was yet another important resolve that Ratan Tata announced soon after the terrorist attack had been quelled. Ratan said that he had decided to work on providing relief and rehabilitation for all victims of the terrorist attacks, which had occurred at many locations across Mumbai. He mentioned that he would set up a vehicle through which such help and relief would be provided to the family of every single person who had been killed and to the injured.

Shrinivas recalls that there were a few senior executives standing near Ratan Tata when he made this announcement. One of them whispered softly to Ratan that they were in touch with police headquarters, but did not know the number of people killed or wounded, or the extent of damage. Perhaps this executive was concerned that the commitment Ratan was making could potentially turn out to be a very large financial obligation since there was no estimate yet of the casualties.

Shrinivas was standing nearby, so he heard Ratan Tata's response to that executive in his soft and measured voice. He recalls that Ratan said something like this (note: these are not the exact words Ratan used but are Shrinivas's recollection after many years): 'So what? Please gather all the data. This city of Mumbai has given us so much. Now, the city is in pain. We have to reach out and stand by it.'

In other words, Ratan Tata was clear that the Tata group would do what was required to provide help and support to the family of every victim across the city, not just employees of the Taj Hotel or the Tata group. He made this commitment despite not knowing the quantum of financial resources that would be required, simply because he instinctively thought it was the right thing to do. This was the emotion of care and compassion overriding any other logical or economic considerations.

This was also the origin of the Taj Public Service Welfare Trust (TPSWT), which was established to provide immediate help to all victims of the terror attacks—including the public, police, firemen, security forces, employees of the Taj and of all other establishments. The announcement of the establishment of this trust included these moving words: 'This is the time for us to conquer despair with compassion. And keep the light of humanity burning bright.' I do not know if these words were crafted or finalized by Ratan Tata, but they certainly reflected his spirit and his resolve.

In fact, Ratan Tata, working closely with KK, personally ensured that the trust was established very quickly, within the next fifteen days. Right at the start of this exercise, he called for a meeting with the CEOs of some major Tata companies and with the senior management of the Taj, where he emphasized the need to begin relief work immediately. 'We have no time to lose,' he is reported to have told the CEOs, 'They are suffering, and we have to start work right away.' Several Tata companies contributed quickly and generously to build the corpus of funds for TPSWT.

TPSWT offered funds for relief and rehabilitation of every victim, having first taken proactive steps to identify the victims and their families across the city. Six relief centres were opened immediately in different areas of Mumbai such as Colaba, Byculla, Andheri, Chembur and Borivili, where food and first aid were provided. These centres were kept open for around six months after the attack. TPSWT helped the injured promptly with their medical expenses, including, in some cases, for surgeries that were required.

Shrinivas recalls that Ratan Tata and KK put great urgency to this effort. They were constantly impatient with progress, and insistent that help be provided promptly. At review meetings with the senior leadership of the Taj, Ratan made it clear that he wanted action fast and without any lapse in time. Ensuring that appropriate help was provided promptly necessitated a detailed but quick need-assessment survey. This was undertaken with expert inputs from the Tata Institute of Social Sciences.

Help to the victims thereafter took many forms, ranging from upfront subsistence cash payments to many families from marginalized backgrounds, to getting children from these families back to school, to providing employment. In several cases, the trust funded the affected people or families to establish small businesses which would take care of their future livelihoods.

For instance, Shrinivas recalls one specific instance where a paan wallah in Colaba had received a bullet injury in his shoulder, and in his absence, his small shop had closed down. The trust took care of his medical treatment and also assisted him in setting up a new paan shop. This is just one amongst many such stories of rehabilitation.

The trust also took responsibility for the education of forty-six children of the victims, thus enabling them to secure their own futures and the lives of their family members. In many cases, skills training was provided as a first step to employment for over ninety people from the families of victims—this happened in the training centre at Taj Lands End Hotel at Bandra. For the affected families, post-trauma counselling was also offered.

Such generous outreach and help was perhaps without precedent, but Ratan Tata's singular objective was to extend help to every victim. Nothing less was acceptable to him.

In addition to the relief work across Mumbai, he also applied himself to the task of taking care of the families of all fourteen employees of the Taj who had lost their lives during the attack. Shrinivas recalls KK telling him, 'Chairman [Ratan Tata] would like to meet the families of all these employees. If the spouse or mother are outside Mumbai, please arrange for their air tickets. If they want to bring family members along, we should agree to that.'

Ratan Tata personally met these families, one by one, in a large suite at the Taj President Hotel. He spent time with them, listening to them, conveying his condolences but also reassuring them that they would be taken care of. These were emotionally intense conversations, but Ratan had decided to sit through each of them. Also present in these meetings along with Ratan were Shrinivas, KK and Raymond Bickson (the then managing director of the Taj).

Shrinivas remembers many of those meetings until today. One such meeting, he recalls, was with Sunu Varghese, whose husband Thomas had been a senior steward at the Taj, and who had lost his life to terrorists' bullets. She was accompanied by members of her family.

When she saw Ratan Tata, she began sobbing. He reassured her and said, 'You are part of the Taj family as long as you are alive. We will take care of you.'

Ratan then waited for her to speak. She took courage and told him how proud she was of her husband, his commitment and work ethic, and how excited Thomas had been to serve his customers. She told him how proud she was that her husband had laid down his life for such a wonderful institution. She said she wanted to put up Thomas's portrait in her sitting room so that both her sons could see him, remember him and follow the values that he had stood for.

After Sunu Varghese said this and left the room, Ratan Tata's eyes turned wet. There was total silence for around half a minute. Then, he looked at his senior colleagues and said, 'How do you explain this? She stands so tall in front of us.' Shrinivas recalls that Ratan's voice had completely choked at that point.

Ratan Tata interacted similarly with each of the families. He reassured each of them that they would be part of the Tata and Taj families throughout their lives. And he mentioned that other than bringing to life the person who had passed away, he was there to make anything else available to them.

After many of these meetings had concluded, Ratan turned to Shrinivas and asked him, 'How do you propose to take care of these families, Mr Shrinivas?'

Shrinivas had prepared a detailed document, which he recalls had seven or eight specific proposals—such as an upfront death relief benefit to the family, pension to the spouse for their lifetime, taking care of the family's medical requirements, bearing the educational expenses of children until a specified age, providing a job to a family member if there was an employable family member, waiving off of any loans provided by the company and providing counselling services. Shrinivas had also listed out in the statement the one-time and recurring cost impact of implementing these proposals.

He handed over that document to Ratan Tata. Ratan read through the entire statement in detail and put it aside without any expression on his face. Around half an hour later, he picked up the statement once again, turned to KK and Shrinivas and said, 'This is the minimum we have to do in any case. But we have to do more than this. What more can we do?'

Shrinivas recalls that as the HR head of the Taj, he had actually been somewhat anxious wondering whether he had gone overboard in putting forward all these proposals. Now, he heard Ratan say exactly the opposite, that even more should be done. Shrinivas says that he saw at that moment what genuine empathy and care was all about, and he adds, 'For me, that was a defining moment of leadership.' The document was duly reworked, with additional proposals.

There are so many moving stories of how these families were supported and rehabilitated. You can read many more of these details in the book *The Taj at Apollo Bunder* authored by Charles Allen and Sharada Dwivedi, and also in Thomas Mathew's comprehensive biography of Ratan Tata.

But pause here for a moment and consider the many actions that Ratan Tata took during this period, including standing on the pavements outside the Taj for nearly three days, the immediate setting up of the TPSWT to help in the relief and rehabilitation of victims across Mumbai, the multiple measures implemented promptly by the TPSWT, interacting personally with families of all Taj employees who had lost their lives, and the finalization of a thoughtful and generous proposal for these families of the Taj.

Ratan took all these actions, many of them without precedent, because he believed that these were the right things to do. He was personally deeply impacted by the 26/11 attacks, even as he put his heart and soul into ensuring that the Tata group displayed true care and compassion in its response.

A Strike at NELCO

One of Ratan Tata's first senior leadership roles in the Tata group was at NELCO. In 1971, Ratan was appointed as the director in charge of the National Radio and Electronics Company, better known as NELCO. This was an ailing and loss-making electronics company, and Ratan inherited a difficult set of challenges when he began his stint here.

Raju Bhinge, who later rose to become the managing director of the Tata Strategic Management Group (TSMG), was a young member of Ratan Tata's team at NELCO in those early years. Bhinge recalls that when Ratan took charge, NELCO lagged far behind the market leaders, Philips and Murphy, in terms of product relevance and range. Ratan Tata took bold steps to recruit competent technical staff and rectify these product issues. He defined a clear direction for the company. Between 1972 and 1975, NELCO grew its market share significantly and also turned profitable. However, in 1975, there was a recession after the declaration of Emergency, and NELCO's financials came under pressure.

Bhinge narrates a compelling story of firmness and care from this time period, specifically from around the year 1980, when NELCO ran into a serious industrial relations problem and a lockout in the factory. The company had a workforce of around 1000 people at that time, many of them employed in the factory at Andheri in Mumbai, where radios and other electronic products were manufactured. Two of the manufacturing shops in this factory—the tool room and the workshop—were staffed primarily by men. On the other hand, the radio assembly lines consisted mainly of women employees.

The workers' unions were dominated by the men, and this resulted in a situation where the women employees were often intimidated by the men. The women did not have much of a say in many matters, including discussions between the union and the management. They were also very uncomfortable with the constant intimidation.

The employees' union had submitted a charter of demands to the management, and these were tabled to Ratan Tata and the leadership team of NELCO. Some of these demands were unreasonable, and this led to a disagreement between the union and management. Initially, the situation was peaceful, though there was tension in the air. However, matters turned nasty when some male employees began indulging in indiscipline, and there were reports of physical violence, including things in the factory getting broken and an incident where an officer was slapped by a union leader.

Ratan Tata, who had been patient for some time, felt that such violence was unacceptable and untenable. In consultation with his managers he decided to declare a lockout in the factory. Ratan was personally very pained at doing this. Nonetheless, he thought that this short-term step was essential to bring back discipline to the factory, which was very important for the company's long-term stability and growth.

Ensuring a steady supply of products to the market was essential to the company's survival. Therefore, in view of the lockout, Ratan and his team took a quick decision to outsource production, which enabled some supplies, though not the full quantities required.

Ratan Tata also took a very clear and principled stand with the union on their charter of demands. Most importantly, he also informed the union that he would not permit the male employees of the tool room and workshop departments to ever again intimidate the women in the workforce. To ensure this, both these departments would have to necessarily be relocated to a new factory premises located at a considerable distance, so that the women in the assembly units could continue to work comfortably at the existing factory in Andheri.

Ratan did this because he had developed a clear view that the women employees were uncomfortable and unhappy with the continuing intimidation by the men. For him, their comfort was important and a priority, alongside all the other issues under negotiation.

Eventually, the lockout at NELCO lasted for as long as seven months. But Ratan Tata did not back down from his condition that the two departments which were staffed by men would be relocated to a new place. In fact, this became a big sticking point during the negotiations. Ratan was also keen that all the other demands be resolved in a fair manner, keeping in mind the future interests of both the company and its workers.

Bhinge remembers that Ratan Tata's firm stance led to a precarious existence for those seven months. Bhinge himself was heading the accounts department in those days, and during those months he was working from an office located in Colaba in South Mumbai. From here, he admired the clear position that Ratan had taken but often wondered how long the impasse would continue.

Eventually, an agreement was reached with the union. As an integral part of this agreement, the tool room and the workshop would be relocated to a new factory premises in Vashi in Navi Mumbai, which was quite far away and across the harbour. On the other hand, the assembly unit, which employed most of the women, would continue to remain in Andheri.

As a result, when the factory reopened after the lockout, the women employees were in a happy situation. They came back immediately to work, reassured that their interests and comfort had been taken care of, and knowing that they would not be subjected to intimidation in the future. Ratan Tata had done what he thought was the right thing to do, notwithstanding the pain involved.

Operators at the Tata Indica Plant

I would like to end this chapter on care and compassion with a small but touching story that I heard at the Pune factory of Tata Motors many years ago, while researching the inspiring tale of the Tata Indica, India's first indigenous car. This story made a huge impact on me, and it has remained vivid in my mind since then.

To make an indigenous Indian car was a dream that Ratan Tata cherished and led, and the Tata Indica was a product of this dream. This lovely car was launched in 1998, and was manufactured in a new plant that had just been established in Pune. Manufacturing cars was new to Tata Motors. Operators for the assembly lines in the factory had been recruited from small towns in Maharashtra such as Kolhapur and Ahmednagar. They were young men, typically in their twenties, who had just completed their apprenticeships.

These operators were excited with their new role in the Indica plant, but, at the same time, it took a lot of rigorous training for them to get skilled at their job. Some of them have narrated to me how it took them eight full days to assemble the first Indica car. Goaded by a sense of urgency and a desire to fulfil consumers' orders, the rate of manufacture increased rapidly from one car per day to 100 to 300.

Ratan Tata used to visit the Indica manufacturing facilities quite often. On one such early visit, he noticed operators fixing the rear strut of the car manually. The operator would have to bend up and down 600 times to complete this operation on 300 cars each day.

Ratan was unhappy when he saw this. He called his managers immediately. 'How can we expect our men to do this throughout their lives?' he asked them. 'Surely it will damage their health. We must provide an automation solution, on priority.'

Ratan was firm on this requirement, and he urged that the solution be put together as quickly as possible. The engineering department rose to the occasion to develop a fixture to semi-automate this operation. This made life incredibly easier for the operators, who remember this fondly even today.

What matters most to them is that their chairman cared for their welfare by noticing the manual operation they were undertaking, thinking spontaneously about the impact this would have on their health, and ensuring that the required automation solution was put in place. Because, for Ratan Tata, this was simply the right thing to do.

9

Respect for People

One of Ratan Tata's distinguishing characteristics was the grace and respect with which he treated the people with whom he interacted. Whether he was interacting with a managing director or a pantry assistant, Ratan would typically be courteous to the extreme. For him, respect for people was his default approach, perhaps because this came naturally to him, but also because he thought this was the right thing to do.

Ishaat Hussain reflects on this aspect of Ratan Tata's personality by using a Persian word.

'The word I would use to describe Ratan Tata is *tehzeeb*,' says Ishaat. 'Tehzeeb is an Urdu word that means several good things all combined together. It means respect, culture, proper behaviour towards everyone, good manners. It also means social grace, politeness and refinement. There is no single word in English which can convey all this with such precision.'

Ishaat goes on to speak about how the Persian courts of yore laid great emphasis on manners and courtesy in dealing with people, as contrasted with the rough or transactional approaches of some other historical dynasties. As he speaks, I can almost imagine that he sees Ratan Tata as one of those Persian kings or nobles, insofar as tehzeeb is concerned. Quite interestingly, such a comparison would not be completely out of line, because Ratan is a Parsi, and his ancestors did indeed come to the Indian subcontinent from Persia (which is now Iran).

Ishaat goes on to say, 'Ratan Tata came from an elite family which was cultured, well-mannered and highly regarded in social circles. He was born into a respectful environment, was brought up by his grandmother, who was a very dignified and respectful lady herself. This upbringing would surely have had an impact in shaping Ratan's respect for everyone he dealt with.'

Ishaat then concludes this conversation by pointing out one more nuanced aspect of Ratan Tata's respect for other people. 'He believed in human dignity. One of the things he would say very often to us was: Never impinge on a person's dignity. It is this belief that led to his courteous and humble demeanour.'

Ratan Tata's respect for other people was visible in so many of his actions. For instance, I have read about how he would take care to respond personally to everyone who wrote to him, notwithstanding the large amount of mail that he would receive, as chairman of Tata Sons. I know of many people who were delighted and overawed to get a signed reply from him. At the root of this urge to respond to every letter was his respect for the person who had taken the effort to write to him.

Even in cases where Ratan was displeased with some work or development, or if something had gone wrong, he would be firm but never raise his voice, shout or use harsh words. This also reflected his respectful approach, and his belief that he should never hurt a person's dignity, regardless of the matter at hand. In fact, in many such cases, people who have interacted extensively with Ratan have mentioned that it was the steely look in his eye and his pursed lips that would indicate his unhappiness.

I recall a meeting where I had been called by Ratan Tata to explain a specific official matter which was causing some concern. By then, I was already a senior officer in the

Tata group, but I had not had the opportunity to interact with Ratan Tata very often. So I did not know what to expect when I walked into his office with all the relevant papers in my hands. Would I get a dressing-down from him or would I have to listen to a few tough words if he felt that what we had done was incorrect or inadequate? But what happened was quite different.

Ratan invited me courteously to sit down and requested me to brief him on the subject. There was one other person in the room with us. He listened to me carefully and silently. When I concluded my submission after around ten minutes, he simply looked at me, conveyed his advice briefly and then said, 'We should do what is right, Harish', in his soft but firm voice. I walked out of his office with clear directional advice and, equally importantly, with my dignity intact.

The stories in this chapter highlight a few different ways through which Ratan Tata showed his respect for people.

Late for a Meeting with Ratan Tata

Sidharth Sharma is the general counsel at Tata Sons. He has been in this leadership role since October 2021. As the highest-ranking legal official of the company, he deals with a wide range of important matters. Sidharth has had a long professional association with the Tata group, starting as a trainee in the group legal team which he now leads. For a few years in the course of his career, he had transitioned to pursue solo law practice in New Delhi, where he advised and acted for the Tata group in several key legal matters.

This story goes back to the times of the COVID-19 pandemic, specifically June 2020. Offices were closed to ensure that there would be no spread of the virus, and most office-based professionals were working from their homes. Courts of law had also shifted to working by virtual mode, over video calls. Just before the lockdown had commenced, Sidharth Sharma happened to be at his ancestral home in Chapra in the state of Bihar. From there, he had gone across to his wife's native village in Madhubani, which is located close to India's border with Nepal. By then, a complete lockdown came into force, and Sidharth continued working virtually from the village in Madhubani.

It was during that time that he received a message saying that Ratan Tata would like to meet him over a video call for a discussion on a specific and urgent legal matter. Ratan Tata was at that time chairman of Tata Trusts and chairman emeritus of Tata Sons. Sidharth had been in touch with Ratan on related subjects for the past several months, and he duly prepared himself for the upcoming video meeting.

Sidharth recalls receiving a video meeting link from Ratan Tata's office for this discussion. At the appointed date and time, he tried to log into the meeting using his laptop. However, the internet and telephone connectivity in the small town of Madhubani was not very robust. Therefore, unfortunately for Sidharth, he could not dial into the meeting despite several attempts.

Sidharth was getting increasingly concerned because he could picture Ratan Tata at the other end in Mumbai, waiting for him to join. Ratan was India's tallest business leader, an icon to millions of Indians. People eagerly waited for even a brief appointment or a simple selfie with him. He was already at an advanced age of eighty-four years. And here was Sidharth, keeping Ratan waiting, because he could not dial into an internet video call.

Sidharth felt both anxious and helpless, as he kept trying. Finally, after a delay of fifteen minutes, he got lucky—the internet connection started working well, and he logged into the call. He could see that Ratan Tata was still there on the other side, waiting. But Sidharth was disturbed and wondered what Ratan Tata would think about him after he had kept him waiting for a full fifteen minutes. Would this be seen as unprofessional behaviour, and would he be upset? Would Sidharth lose the respectful relationship he had built with Mr Tata? Therefore, he framed some apologetic sentences with which he could begin the discussion.

However, as soon as the video call connected, Sidharth saw that Ratan Tata was not upset in any manner. On the other hand, he was looking quite calm and composed. His office had told him that Sidharth was away in his hometown. Ratan turned to Sidharth and his first words were as soft as ever, 'If you have any difficulty in connecting, we can reschedule this call.'

Clearly, Ratan Tata had sensed that something had inadvertently gone wrong, and he wanted to make Sidharth feel at ease. This was driven by his sense of kindness, and also his respect for Sidharth as a professional. Perhaps Ratan did not want Sidharth to feel that he had done something wrong or impinge on his professional worth in any manner.

Therefore, there was no expression of annoyance, no asking Sidharth why he was late, and absolutely no other subtext which would have made Sidharth feel small or guilty of wasting his time or being unprofessional. Just a nice statement expressing care. That was Ratan's way of being compassionate and protecting the dignity of the other individual.

Sidharth says that Ratan Tata's opening sentence wiped out his fear and anxiety completely. On the other hand, if Ratan Tata had delved directly into the subject of the discussion without this initial comment, Sidharth would have felt internally uneasy throughout the meeting and thereafter as well.

'That was Ratan Tata,' says Sidharth. 'Always respectful, always graceful. He was always on time to every meeting.' Sidharth recalls instances when Mr Tata had to reschedule a discussion, and he would do so well in advance. If the rescheduled meeting happened to be on a weekend, Ratan Tata would often telephone personally and inform him. While calling Sidharth to meet him, Mr Tata would always ask if the time was convenient. 'He did not need to do that', says Sidharth.

Sidharth continues, 'Mr Tata was always neatly dressed, always graceful and courteous to others in the room. I have never ever heard him raise his voice. Sometimes, his body language would reflect his unhappiness, but never his voice.

Ratan Tata practised those qualities and courtesies every day. That made him a great person, loved and respected by so many. I was very fortunate to get the opportunity to work and interact with Mr Tata closely.'

Sidharth concludes by saying, 'It is easy to admire Mr Ratan Tata but difficult to emulate him, and be like him in our everyday lives.'

Anatomy of a Phone Call

B. Muthuraman was managing director and CEO of Tata Steel between 2001 and 2009, and thereafter vice chairman of the company until 2014. During this time, he reported directly to Ratan Tata, who was the chairman of the company. This was a period when Tata Steel witnessed significant growth domestically through the expansion of its steel-making facility in Jamshedpur. In addition, it also expanded overseas through acquisitions including Tata Steel Thailand and Tata Steel Europe (earlier known as Corus). Muthu (as Muthuraman was referred to by his colleagues) was the CEO driving this transformation, with guidance from Ratan and the board of the company.

Once, in the year 2007, Muthu and his leadership team were in the midst of discussing a complex commercial deal with another company. Supporting Muthu in these discussions was Kaushik Chatterjee, the CFO of Tata Steel. Discussions with the other party had been continuing for around a month. Ratan Tata and Muthuraman held different views on the proposed deal, hence reaching a decision required further consultations.

Eventually, the deadline for taking a decision on the deal came close. Muthuraman, as CEO, had to convey a final decision to the other company, indicating to them whether Tata Steel would go ahead with the deal or not. Muthuraman had committed to that company that he would revert to them latest by 10 p.m. on a particular day.

On the morning of that day, Muthuraman woke up and proceeded to his office on the third floor of Bombay House. He knew that that day was what corporate circles referred to as 'crunch time', a critical point in time when an important decision would have to be made, one way or the other. And he also knew that whatever be the decision to be conveyed to the other party, he would need the concurrence of his chairman, Ratan Tata.

Ratan Tata was away in Delhi on that date for an important meeting, so an in-person meeting between

Ratan and Muthuraman was unfortunately not possible. However, Ratan spoke to Muthuraman on the phone and told him, 'Muthu, don't worry. I am coming back to Mumbai later this evening. I will be landing in Mumbai at 7 p.m., and should be in my car at 7.30 p.m., on my way back home. I will call you from my mobile phone around that time.'

Muthuraman waited in his office that evening, accompanied by his CFO, Kaushik. It was a tense wait for him because he knew that the deadline was coming close. However, promptly at 7.30 p.m., Ratan Tata called.

He said, 'Muthu, what have you thought about this, what would you like to do?'

Muthuraman put forward his point of view. Ratan listened, and then put forward his own point of view, which continued to be at variance to what Muthu felt. There appeared to be no meeting ground.

Muthuraman felt that he should explain once more how moving ahead with his view on the deal would benefit the company. Therefore, he responded to Ratan Tata on the telephone and spoke again about the benefits of what he was suggesting as the way forward. It was not easy to be persistent in that manner, when the person at the other end was the chairman of the Tata group. However, Muthu felt that this was the right thing to do in his role as CEO of the company, particularly because he had high levels of conviction about his point of view.

Finally, Ratan Tata spoke. He said, 'Muthu, if you want to pursue this line of action, please go ahead and decide, but please leave me out of the decision-making process.'

Ratan's voice came through clearly over the telephone, and Muthuraman could sense his irritation. He was perhaps irritated that his CEO was insisting on a certain path ahead, and was unwilling to change his point of view.

At that exact moment, just after Ratan Tata had concluded his statement, the phone went dead. Completely dead. As Muthuraman listened, there was silence on the other side.

The first thought that occurred to Muthuraman was that Ratan Tata had got so irritated with his (Muthu's) unchanging stance, that 'he had banged the phone down on me'. For people in positions of power, this is not an uncommon thing to do, to display displeasure or to bring a conversation that involves disagreement to an abrupt close.

Muthuraman felt very bad at that moment. Had he hurt Ratan Tata with his persistence? Had he done the right thing in continuing to argue in favour of his point of view? It was not a good feeling at all, to think that one had displeased the chairman so much that he had so brusquely disconnected the call.

Even as Muthuraman was wrestling with these emotions, Kaushik Chatterjee asked him, 'Sir, what do we do now?'

Muthuraman heard him, but frankly he did not know what to do. The deadline was only a couple of hours away. The chairman had asked him to decide but had also told him in an irritated tone to leave him out of the decision-making process.

For a couple of minutes, Muthuraman was struggling with all these thoughts. But even as he was in this frame of mind, he heard his phone ring. It was Ratan Tata on the line once again. Muthu wondered what Ratan would say now.

'Muthu,' Ratan began, 'I rang you up not for any discussion on the deal. You can decide on that. But you should not think that I banged the phone down on you. I did not bang the phone down. My car went over a big road bump, and there was a sudden call drop (on my mobile phone).'

Muthuraman recalls that he was not just amazed, he was moved as he heard Ratan speak. Here was the chairman of the Tata group, calling him back just to clarify that the call had dropped and was not deliberately disconnected.

Muthuraman says, 'He did not have to call me back to say this, but he did. He intuitively sensed what I was going through, the discomfort I would have been feeling. And he wanted to tell me not to get perturbed, not to misinterpret why the call had closed down. This was a call driven by his respect and care for his colleague.'

Muthuraman goes on to say, using an evocative turn of phrase, 'With that call, Ratan Tata was putting his arms around me, all the way from his car.'

They also then went on to discuss the deal. Eventually, they reached a common point of view, which was then communicated to the other party well in time of the 10 p.m. deadline.

Muthuraman concludes this story by saying, 'That second call was not about the transaction at all. It was a call about human grace, respect and care. It brought tears to my eyes. It was an amazing gesture.'

Muthuraman narrated this story to me in 2025, eighteen years after it had actually occurred. Yet, even as he completed his narration, he began crying. And he said, 'I was reimagining that entire scene just now, and tears are still rolling down my eyes. What an amazing person Ratan Tata was.'

That is the power of respect for your colleagues, of care for human beings who work with you. Ratan Tata did what he thought was the right thing to do, in making that second phone call to Muthuraman. And through gestures such as this, he touched a million hearts.

Saying Goodbye at the Door

In 2024, a few months before Ratan Tata passed away, he asked to see Ishaat Hussain. Ratan was eighty-seven years old and not in the best of health. He lived in a little bungalow in Colaba in South Mumbai, known as 'Halekai', a Hawaiian word that means 'home by the sea'.

Ishaat recalls that Ratan and he had a good and informal discussion on that day, and then it was time for him to leave. So he said goodbye to Ratan and began walking towards the door of the house. However, as he did this, he saw Ratan get up and walk towards the door as well.

Ishaat could see that Ratan was having some difficulty in walking, and he tried to dissuade him from coming to the door. 'Sir, please don't take the trouble,' Ishaat said, but Ratan Tata responded, 'No, no, I will come with you.'

'This was not easy for Ratan,' Ishaat says. 'If you have been to his house, you know that there is a climb from the seating area to the door. It is not a flat surface but a gentle climb. The entry to the house is virtually at the level of the first floor. I could see that Ratan was having great difficulty in walking up. Yet he insisted on coming right up to the door.'

As Ishaat exited the house, he waved goodbye to Ratan Tata, who was at the doorway. Then, as he got into his car and drove away, he looked back. To his surprise, Ratan was still there. So Ishaat waved at him once again. In fact, Ratan continued waiting at the door until Ishaat's car left the house and drove away.

'This was extraordinary, and he need not have done this at all,' says Ishaat, as he goes on to speak about Ratan Tata's insistence on proper behaviour in all his interactions. 'Ratan Tata personified respect and good manners.'

Many other colleagues who visited Ratan at his home have narrated almost identical stories to me. He was very courteous, often to a fault. When he returned from his overseas travels, he would often write personal letters of thanks to chauffeurs and staff who had served him during these visits.

These are simple gestures of courtesy, but they are rare in today's world, particularly amongst leaders who occupy positions of power. For Ratan Tata, they were integral to his personality. He carried himself with grace and simplicity, and he was respectful in his behaviour towards others. He treated people with dignity because he thought that this was the right thing to do.

10

Meeting Every Commitment

Many people in positions of power make commitments to others. But not all of them honour every commitment they make. Sometimes, this is because of unanticipated roadblocks. At other times, it is because the commitment has been made somewhat casually.

For Ratan Tata, however, meeting every commitment that he had made, notwithstanding any challenges, was a defining characteristic. For him, there were no shades of grey. It was simply a matter of ensuring that if a promise had been made, it had to be kept.

Having said that, he would sometimes think for a long time before making any such promise, particularly on key matters. People who have worked closely with him have described how he would often come to a firm decision only after several rounds of discussions, lots of back and forth, and after letting the matter brew in his mind for days together. However, once he reached a firm conclusion, he would commit himself to a path of action and ensure that he honoured that particular commitment fully.

In matters that involved either a legal or moral commitment, he was always clear that such a commitment needed to be upheld at any cost. For him, this was integral to the promise of the Tata brand. The story of Tata Finance, which has been narrated in detail earlier in this book, is a case in point. In Ratan Tata's mind, there was a moral commitment from the Tata group to all depositors, which needed to be met, no matter what the financial consequences. This was the simple reason why he stood up and made a public statement during the early days of this unfortunate episode that every rupee of every depositor's funds would be safe.

Yet another illustration of Ratan Tata's resolve to deliver on every promise was his absolute commitment to fulfilling the Tata group's obligation to NTT Docomo of Japan, which arose consequent to the Japanese company's exit from the Tata Docomo venture. Ratan was determined that a solution to this vexing issue should be found, and appeared satisfied only after the

Tatas eventually discharged this obligation in 2017. This story has been covered in detail in many other publications, so I am choosing not to narrate it here once again.

While examples such as Tata Finance and Tata Docomo are in the business space, and involve legal, moral or financial commitments made on the high tables of corporate life, Ratan Tata was equally relentless about meeting personal commitments that he made from time to time. If he had committed that he would meet a person or visit a certain location, he would actively strive to do this without fail.

Dr J.J. Irani, who worked closely with Ratan Tata for several years, has written about him, 'I have seen him travel the world when in physical distress just to ensure that a commitment he had made is met, where his physical presence would make a difference to the future of the group.'

The stories that follow bring to life one of Ratan Tata's abiding principles: A promise is a promise. This is not just an inspiring statement, it is a rallying call that can motivate each of us to honour the commitments we make in our own lives.

A Man of His Word

Atul Bhide is an entrepreneur turned development sector professional. He lives in Thane, near Mumbai. In 2011, he founded Om Audio Books, with a focus on creating exceptional audiobooks for listeners.

His first major project under this venture was the creation of an audio version of the biography of Dr Verghese Kurien, who had revolutionized India's dairy production through Amul. This biography had already been published as a printed book, under the title *I Too Had a Dream*. Now, Atul wanted to convert it into a superb audiobook to extend its reach and multiply its impact. He had also decided on a catchy title for this audiobook: *The Man Who Made the Elephant Dance*.

The printed biography contained a beautiful foreword written by Ratan Tata. Hence, Atul thought that the audiobook should include this foreword in Ratan Tata's own voice. It would be a perfect start. The rest of the book would be narrated by the famous cinema and theatre actor Tom Alter, who had agreed to undertake this project.

However, Atul had no contacts within the Tata group. None of his close relatives or friends worked at Tata.

He also knew that Ratan Tata, as chairman of the Tata group, had a very busy schedule. Therefore, obtaining his agreement to record this foreword was a very long shot. Nonetheless, he decided to write to Ratan with this request.

He did so on 8 November 2011, laying out the context for this project and requesting him (Ratan) to be part of it. In particular, could he please read out the foreword, which would be recorded and used in the audio book?

Atul did not know whether he would receive a response to this letter. He imagined that Ratan Tata would perhaps be receiving many, many varied requests. In any case, Ratan did not know him. So, while Atul fervently wished for the best, he did not harbour high hopes.

Around a week later, on 16 November, Atul was driving in Mumbai, from Tardeo back home to Thane. He recalls that day quite vividly. As he drove through the city, he heard an email notification ping on his mobile phone. Overtaken by curiosity, he parked his car near the Sion junction and looked at his mail. It was an email from Ratan Tata's office, which requested him to refer to the attached letter.

For some reason, Atul was unable to open the attachment. But he was impatient to know whether Ratan Tata had agreed to participate. So he telephoned home and requested his wife to open the attached letter and read it out to him. He could not contain his excitement as his wife did so. It turned out to be a personal note signed by Ratan Tata himself. Ratan said he was pleased to know about the project, and also agreed to do the audio recording. He suggested that Atul stay in touch with his office to fix up a suitable date, perhaps sometime in December.

Atul was ecstatic. His dream was about to come true: an audiobook about a national icon, Dr Verghese Kurien, with a foreword in the voice of another national icon, Ratan Tata! He also spoke to Mrs Kurien and shared the good news with her. She was equally elated.

However, as December dawned, Atul received a message from Ratan Tata's office mentioning that Ratan would be very busy during December, and hence the audio recording would stand postponed. Atul had seen the media announcement during the last week of November of Cyrus Mistry having been appointed successor to Ratan Tata. He therefore realized that this was perhaps an extraordinarily busy time for Ratan, as he would be travelling with Cyrus to many offices of the Tata group.

Before Atul could fully realize the passage of time, it was March 2012. He was getting somewhat worried now about when Ratan Tata's audio recording would happen. Therefore, around mid-March, he decided to visit Ratan's office to inquire about the appointment, and also to hand over a prototype of the audiobook. It was proposed that the cover of the audiobook would contain a photograph of Ratan Tata, and Atul needed his approval before proceeding.

Within a week, Atul received a reply from Ratan Tata. The reply acknowledged receipt of the prototype and went on to say: 'I apologize for not having been able to indicate a time for recording my foreword for the book due to my travel commitments. I am scheduled to be travelling through the next two weeks but would be pleased to meet you on my return in early April. My office will contact you to coordinate a mutually convenient date for the recording. With regards, Ratan Tata.'

Atul was amazed when he read this letter. Here was the chairman of India's largest industrial group apologizing to him for a postponement in the date of the recording. Speaking in 2025, over thirteen years later, Atul says with emotion in his voice, 'This was unbelievable. He was a national icon, with so many commitments. Atul Bhide is a common man, no one in front of him. And yet he wrote me a personal letter of apology. That is the greatness of Ratan Tata.'

In line with Ratan Tata's commitment, his office provided a time on 3 April for the audio recording. On that day, Atul, accompanied by his recording engineer, entered Bombay House, the headquarters of the Tata group, and headed up to the stately boardroom on the fourth floor. When he entered, he was overcome with a sense of history and could not bring himself to sit down.

'How could I sit in these chairs which had been used by legends over the decades?' says Atul, as he recollects that moment.

Ratan Tata entered the boardroom, accompanied by his close aide Ajay Kumar. He was dressed in a grey suit, a light blue shirt and a blue tie that sported checks on it. He sat down, began speaking and asked the engineer to confirm whether his voice was coming through fine. After receiving this confirmation, he went ahead and completed the entire audio recording of the foreword, reading out from the printed book. Then he asked the engineer whether the recording was to his satisfaction. The engineer affirmed this and Ratan Tata thanked him.

Ratan Tata thus fulfilled the commitment he had made to a man he did not know, notwithstanding all the other pressures on his time during a particularly busy time of leadership transition. This was not a commitment necessitated by any legal or business agreement; it was not a commitment to some high functionary, yet in Ratan's mind it was as important as any other.

Thereafter, Ratan shook hands with Atul, asked him a few questions about his profession and his family, extending warm courtesies, rather than leaving immediately like some important people are prone to do. He also agreed to a group photograph with Atul and his recording engineer. After one picture had been clicked, Mr Tata said, 'Take one more, just to be sure.' He then patted Atul on the back and shook his hand. As they walked towards the elevators, Atul suddenly realized that he was with the one and only Ratan Tata, and sought his blessings.

Atul Bhide left Bombay House that day in an elated but slightly dazed state of mind. He had met Ratan Tata himself, and been treated with such grace and generosity. Here was a man who had not hesitated to apologize, and who had met his personal commitment with such sincerity.

'This is what the Ratan of India was all about,' says Atul, recalling that entire episode. 'He was a man of his word. I have not come across another person like him.'

(Atul Bhide continued to remain in touch with Ratan Tata for several years after this meeting, updating him about key events in his professional and personal life. Ratan Tata replied without fail to each of Atul's email messages over the years. Atul's telling of this entire story was one of the most emotive narrations I have ever heard.)

A Promise Is a Promise

One of Ratan Tata's most cherished dreams, and perhaps his most audacious, was the creation of a small and affordable car that could potentially upgrade millions of middle-class Indians from two-wheeler riders to car owners. The world knows this car as the Nano. Unfortunately, the Nano has not turned out to be a commercial success, primarily because of inappropriate brand positioning and poor marketing. However, this marketing failure does not take away from the fact that the Nano is one of the greatest product innovations to come out of modern India.

Ratan Tata unveiled the Nano at India's Auto Expo in January 2008, with the famous words 'A promise is a promise'. This is the story of that promise made by Ratan, and how he kept it.

This particular slice of the Nano story begins at another auto show, five years earlier: the Geneva Auto Show of 2003. Ratan Tata was present at this event, which was its seventy-third edition. There, he was interviewed by the British newspaper *Financial Times*. During the course of this interview, Ratan mentioned that an affordable car was being considered by Tata Motors. He was then asked about the cost of such a car, and he responded saying that it could be around $2500 (at that time, this was the equivalent of Rs 1 lakh).

This was just a general mention, because the car had not yet been designed or priced at that point in time. The next day, the newspaper carried a report that the Tata group was planning to make a 'Rs 1 lakh car'. This price point thus became a headline, which was not Ratan Tata's intent at all.

Ratan Tata could have refuted this newspaper report. However, as he has said in some subsequent conversations, he felt that the mention and public coverage of the 'Rs 1 lakh' price point was a wonderful thing to have happened, because it provided the team a simple and clear goal which was considered impossible at that time. For Ratan Tata, this was an excellent starting point, because it would challenge all of them hugely and push their thinking beyond the obvious.

This is how the legend of the Rs 1 lakh price point of the Nano took birth. Most automotive industry professionals were sceptical. Some held that a car at this low a price would never be possible. But for Ratan, it was now a firm target. Many people in India began referring to the Nano in local parlance as the 'Lakhtakia' (Rs 1 lakh) car. I recall that there was a great amount of anticipation and excitement in my own friends' circles about what this car would look like, what features it would have, and whether the final price point would actually be Rs 1 lakh.

Within Tata Motors, the Nano team got to work. Starting 2005, the team was led by a bright young engineer, Girish Wagh. He reported to Ravi Kant, who had then just become the managing director of Tata Motors, and he also interacted directly with Ratan Tata on this project. Girish is now the executive director of Tata Motors. Ravi Kant retired many years ago. I interviewed both of them for this book in 2025. There are two points that both of them made to me during our conversations: that Ratan Tata defined targets which were audacious, and once he had set these targets, there was no looking back.

To begin with, a strict cost code had to be defined: every element of the car had to be as cost-effective as possible. There were multiple, long brainstorming sessions on how this could be done. The engineering expertise that the Tata Motors team had gained from earlier marquee projects, such as the Indica and the Ace, also came in very helpful here. Even as Ratan Tata pushed for a smart, modern and user-friendly design of the car which scored high on safety and utility, he was also clear that cost was a key consideration. Nothing that was unnecessary would be included, and the base version of the car in particular would have nothing fancy within it.

Ratan personally involved himself in many important decisions, and his interventions provided key inputs and support to the team who grappled with a multitude of challenges in producing a car that could be priced at the unbelievable figure of Rs 1 lakh.

Girish Wagh recalls that from an engineering perspective, one key challenge was 'to get the engine with the right capacity and configuration. And so we had to redesign it twice, and increase the capacity to get to exactly the right power, which is significantly difficult'.

Indeed, the team started with a 543 cc engine, but when Ratan Tata thought that this did not provide the required acceleration, it was replaced with a 586 cc engine. Ratan felt that this was not good enough either, keeping in mind the likely demands of the Indian consumer. Eventually, a 623 cc engine was crafted, and a final call was taken that this was the correct size for the Nano.

A second challenge, says Wagh, 'was to ensure that the cabin of the car is spacious and safe enough, but also lightweight'.

One of the decisions that the team took to address this challenge and ensure maximum space in the cabin of this small car, without adding weight or cost, was to locate the engine at the rear. This was not common at all amongst cars in India, though rear engines had been used in the past by global car models such as the Volkswagen Beetle and the Porsche 911. This released a lot of space within the Nano, and also gave the car a larger area (crumple zone) that could absorb the impact of any crash.

There were many other design, engineering and cost challenges that had to be constantly navigated to deliver the optimal cost–quality solutions. In addition, during the period of the project, there were significant cost escalations of raw materials which had to be addressed. This put a lot of pressure on the team, which had to keep going back to the drawing board, not once or twice, but several times. Such a situation could potentially lead to frustration or burnout.

Hence, in many ways, the real challenge was not technical, it was human. Here too, Ratan Tata played a key role. Says Wagh, 'The real challenge was to keep the team motivated and remove the fear of failure. It is not easy to redesign such a large and complex aggregate, as also a number of smaller items. Ratan Tata created an environment where there was encouragement for lateral thinking, no fear of failure, and every subsequent experimentation was appreciated. That egged the team on to keep delivering better, better and better.'

Better and better and better. Whether it was the single-piece dashboard, or the development of an appropriate single-blade wiper, the braking system or the development of a cost-effective component supplier network, this is what the Nano team kept pursuing. In many cases, the ideas pursued came from outside the normal boundaries of the automobile ecosystem. Over 8000 ideas were evaluated during the course of this project through three waves of cost-reduction initiatives.

A base model of the Nano was defined for the entry price, and higher-end models with more features were also included in the product range. Throughout all these exercises, Ratan Tata insisted on the right quality for customers without permitting any compromises on cost. The unanticipated move of the factory from its originally planned location of Singur (this story has been narrated earlier in this book) also added to the overall anxiety on costs. But the team derived great strength and motivation from Ratan's strong and unconditional backing. Working through several iterations and going beyond the conventional, the team learnt, step by step, idea by idea, how to make the impossible possible.

As the unveiling and launch of the Nano came close, one of the factors Ratan Tata must have been thinking about was the pricing of the car. In the lovely book *Small Wonder: The Making of the Nano*, published by the Tata Sons Group Publication team in 2010, there is reference to the fact that when Girish Wagh brought up the subject of pricing with Ratan Tata, Ratan listened to him but did not say anything. However, this would undoubtedly have been a live topic in Ratan's mind, particularly given his initial mention of the likely cost of the car being around Rs 1 lakh, which had been plastered all over media. Having said that, this mention was a full five years ago, in 2003. Would this price still hold, after so long?

The answer to this question would only be known publicly on 10 January 2008 at Pragati Maidan in Delhi. The Auto Expo had opened at this vast ground in the national capital. Lakhs of people visited this expo that year—including automobile enthusiasts, business people, government dignitaries, celebrities from various walks of life and ordinary people like you and me. The Auto Expo always had a buzz to it, but this year it had reached the zenith of its popularity, primarily because of the rush of curiosity about one new product which was playing on virtually everyone's mind: Can we get to see the small car from Tata? What would it be like? What would it be priced at?

At around 10 a.m. that morning, the stage was set for the unveiling of the Nano. Hall Number 11, where this car would soon appear, was packed to the hilt. The event began with a pre-recorded message from Ratan Tata, where he spoke about some innovations which had changed the world and also the genesis of the Nano. Then, Ratan drove on stage with the first Nano the world would officially see: a pearly white car.

As he did this, the inspiring musical theme from Stanley Kubrick's *2001: A Space Odyssey* gave him company. This riveting piece of music, inspired by Richard Strauss's tone poem 'Thus Spoke Zarathustra', was apt company for the path-breaking small car. The crowd saw the car drive in and went into raptures. If there were any lingering doubts that a small car at such an affordable price could ever be made, they were washed away by the appearance of the vehicle.

Then, Ratan Tata emerged from the car and began speaking. He spoke about why the car had been named Nano—explaining that this name conveyed both high technology and small size. He then came to the part about the price of the car. The crowd was hanging on to his every word at this stage. He set the preface by explaining that the costs of making the car had gone up significantly since the project had been conceived many years ago.

And then he made the announcement that everyone there, and the entire nation beyond the Auto Expo, had been waiting for. The standard version of the Nano would come with a dealer price of Rs 1 lakh. The crowd broke into huge applause.

Ratan then added the famous words: 'Having said that, I just want to say, that's because a promise is a promise.'

Ratan Tata had redeemed his promise and launched the Nano at Rs 1 lakh, the price point which he had casually mentioned during a newspaper interview five years ago, but which had then defined the target for the entire team and for himself.

It was incredible that despite all the challenges—cutting across unprecedented engineering and design issues, cost escalations and shifting out of the original manufacturing location—Ratan Tata and his team at Tata Motors had still delivered the Nano at this unbelievable price point.

'A promise is a promise' was spoken by Ratan in the context of the pricing of the Nano, but it soon came to represent the man himself. A man who believed in meeting every commitment that he made.

(Unfortunately, the Nano was not a commercial success. Much has been written on this subject over the years. I agree with the analysis which many people have presented, and which Ratan Tata himself has referred to, that it should have been marketed differently. A car is an aspirational purchase, and no one would like to buy a 'cheap' car. Instead, it could have been positioned as a 'stylish and smart small car', without explicit headlining of the price. People would then have discovered for themselves the stunning entry price point of Rs 1 lakh and the incrementally higher price points of the higher-end models. All this is, of course, easily said today with the benefit of hindsight.)

A Meeting on 27/11

On 26 November 2008, Mumbai city was attacked by terrorists of the Lashkar-e-Taiba, who had sailed in from Pakistan. It was one of the most tragic days in the history of the city—166 people were killed and over 300 injured. Some of the locations that were attacked on that day included the Chhatrapati Shivaji Maharaj Train Terminus (formerly known as VT or the Victoria Terminus), the Taj Mahal Palace Hotel, Oberoi Trident Hotel, Nariman House and Leopold Café.

The Taj Mahal Palace Hotel had been created by Jamsetji Tata over a century ago, in 1903. On the night of 26 November, it was under siege as four terrorists entered the hotel and began shooting indiscriminately. This was a totally unprecedented situation. Ratan Tata had rushed to the hotel soon after receiving news of the terror attack. He attempted to enter the hotel, but the police rightly stopped him from doing so.

Ratan then moved to the pavement just outside the Taj. He stood there on the pavement for many hours on the first night of the attack, and for the next three days as well, except for brief breaks to go to his office at Bombay House or home. He felt helpless, but he was determined to show his solidarity with the people who were facing such danger within the hotel. His constant presence there greatly motivated the staff of the Taj.

The story of what happened at the Taj during these 26/11 attacks has been narrated earlier in this book. But here is a little story of what happened on the morning of 27 November—the morning after the attack—which has been narrated to me by R. Gopalakrishnan (Gopal), who worked closely with Ratan Tata for several years. Gopal was, at that time, an executive director at Tata Sons, and a member of the Group Executive Council that had been constituted by Ratan Tata.

Well before the terror attacks happened, Gopal had obtained an appointment to meet Ratan Tata at 10 a.m. on

27 November 2008. He turned up at Ratan Tata's office five minutes early. He knew of the ongoing terror attacks at the Taj that had begun the previous night, but this was a meeting with the group chairman, and he had not received any messages or calls deferring the meeting. So he told himself, 'I must go.'

Gopal says, 'I turned up at five minutes to 10 a.m., and he was there in his office, right on time. He was looking so bleary-eyed, and therefore I asked him, "If you are not in the mood for this meeting, why did you come?"'

Ratan Tata looked at him and responded, 'I had made a commitment to you that I would see you at 10.'

Gopal goes on to say, 'He need not have come to meet me that morning. All of us knew what had happened the night before. It would have been a simple matter for his office or assistant to call me and postpone the meeting. As chairman, he had all the prerogative and liberty to do that.

'This meeting is a very small point but it highlights a big principle. For him, keeping to his word was sacred.'

Gopalakrishnan then requested Ratan Tata to postpone the meeting to another date, given how tired Ratan was that morning. Ratan agreed to this request.

This meeting on the morning of 27/11 highlights an underlying urge that defined Ratan Tata's way of life: if he made a commitment, however large or small, he wanted to keep it, no matter what the circumstances were. And why? Simply because he thought that this was the right thing to do.

11

Four Timeless Learnings from Ratan Tata

Over the past nine chapters, we have examined what 'doing the right thing' meant to Ratan Tata. Eight themes emerged, which appear to have guided Ratan's thinking and decision-making:

1. Being a true custodian of Tata values
2. Putting the nation first
3. Ethical conduct of business
4. Going beyond legal compliance—being morally correct
5. Fostering fairness
6. Care and compassion
7. Respect for people
8. Meeting every commitment

We saw these themes in action through specific stories drawn from Ratan Tata's life. Each of these real-life stories constitutes a case study in itself, with invaluable lessons that can guide each of us in doing the right thing in our own lives.

Just to be clear, these themes have been about Ratan Tata's preoccupation with always doing the right thing. This does not mean or imply that he always succeeded in doing the right thing or achieving the intended results of his actions. Some of his decisions did not yield the required outcomes, and there is scope for a separate book to examine the learnings from these failures. After all, Ratan Tata was human, and, as the well-known saying goes, to err is human. But this does not take away from his constant desire to do what he thought was right.

It is this desire to 'do the right thing' that I have addressed in this book, and which I believe that each of us can learn from. Having explored how Ratan Tata addressed this urge, it would now be worthwhile to ask ourselves: Are there any essential principles that we can adopt if we wish to consistently do the right thing in our own lives?

Some of you may ask me: Why should we want to do this? To all of you who ask this question, my answer would be: simply because most of us wish to lead good and fulfilling lives, and also sleep well at night. Since doing the right thing appears to enable both these objectives, perhaps this is a good direction to pursue.

On a related note, we may never become the chairman of a large industrial group like Ratan Tata was, and we may never reach anywhere close to the iconic status that he attained, but how do we bring this same idea of doing what is right into our own roles, whether we are a marketing manager, a start-up founder, a doctor, a journalist, a professor, a homemaker or a self-employed professional? Because this is a universal idea, not limited by role or stature, and if we adapt it to our own lives, it can benefit each of us.

Four Essential Principles

Based on the thoughts that have evolved in my mind while researching and writing this book, I would like to propose that there are four essential and timeless principles that we can learn from Ratan Tata's pursuit of doing the right thing. These tenets, when considered in aggregate, will guide us towards making the right decisions and taking the right actions in our own lives.

These four principles are:

1. Leading a life of integrity
2. Embracing our roles
3. Displaying humanity
4. Refusing to succumb

Leading a Life of Integrity

Ratan Tata's urge to do the right thing at all times came, first and foremost, from his endeavour to lead a life of integrity.

Integrity is one of the most powerful words in the English language, and it is also one of the most influential concepts that have shaped human civilization. The Cambridge Dictionary defines integrity as 'the quality of being honest and having strong moral principles that you refuse to change'. There are two elements of integrity that leap out from this definition: first, being honest, and second, consistent adherence to some moral principles which are very important to you.

It is because Ratan Tata was an honest man that he refused outright to participate in any dealing or opportunity that involved bribery or corruption. Some of the stories you have read in earlier chapters of this book—such as his pioneering establishment of the Progressive Electoral Trust to bring transparency into the funding of political parties, or his walking away from some business opportunities that potentially involved illegal gratification—illustrate how he put this principle into practice, even if this meant an opportunity loss in economic terms.

In addition to sheer honesty, some key moral principles—such as fairness to all stakeholders, or respect towards the people he interacted with—were very important to Ratan Tata, and his constant urge was to stay true to these values. Some illustrations of this, which we have encountered in this book, include the story of how he responded to the fraud at Tata Finance, his reactions that guided the sale of the Tata group's equity stake in Hitech Drilling and his simple insistence on responding to every letter that he received.

Each of us have similar opportunities in our own lives to practise honesty in all our dealings, and to stay true to our own moral values. While the concept of honesty—being truthful and sincere in our thoughts, statements and actions—is well understood universally, the moral values which are most important to each of us may differ from person to person, or from one society to another. For example, for some people, displaying kindness may be far more important than being scrupulously fair, whereas for others just the opposite may be true. With respect to so many of these moral values, there are no absolute rankings of how we should order them. What is important is that we stay true to the moral values that are most important to us. This requires each of us to identify, in our own minds, the core moral principles that we will never stray from.

When we practise honesty consistently, and also make every effort to stay true to these moral principles which are very important to us, then we naturally move towards making the right choices and doing the right thing. This is not easy to do because the path of integrity is strewn with multiple hurdles and temptations. But the overriding desire to lead a life of integrity is one of the key reasons why Ratan Tata did the right thing, and why we too can do what is right in our own lives.

Embracing Our Roles

Ratan Tata fully embraced his role as chairman of Tata Sons, and then, in later years, as chairman of Tata Trusts. He did not merely pursue these roles as a means of livelihood or as a nine-to-five professional occupation. On the other hand, he subsumed himself into these roles completely. As a result, he considered himself the custodian of the Tata legacy, and he also took to heart the need to contribute to nation-building, which is at the core of the Tata group's philosophy of business. His drive to do what is right for India—whether it be the creation of a network of cancer hospitals, or his strong and objective leadership of the Investment Council of India—was driven, at least in some part, by his complete identification with his role and the responsibilities it placed on him.

Similarly, it is because of Ratan's tight embrace of his role and responsibility that he did what he considered the right things to safeguard the future of the group—whether it be the creation of the Tata Brand Equity and Business Promotion agreement or the battles with the satraps during the early years of his assuming the role, or addressing the succession at Tata Sons. Some of these were not easy or comfortable decisions. Yet he went ahead because he considered them the right actions to protect the future of the Tatas.

Each of us can learn from this approach. If we identify fully with our professional roles, rather than consider our jobs or businesses as mere livelihoods, then we are likely to develop the mindset and the courage to do what is right, notwithstanding how challenging these actions are likely to be. This is true of virtually every role, and it is particularly relevant to any position of leadership, big or small.

Each role comes with its own short-term and long-term responsibilities, and in virtually every role we are a custodian of something or the other—either a product, a brand, a manufacturing facility, a supply chain, a team or, sometimes, an entire business. Living our role to the fullest will enable us to develop the mindset of true custodians, rather than adopting the thinking of short-term occupiers of our seats. This, in turn, will give us the strength to do the right things, just like Ratan Tata did in his role at the Tata group.

Displaying Humanity

For over two decades, Ratan Tata was chairman of Tata Sons, arguably the most powerful and wide-ranging leadership role in corporate India. Thereafter, until the time of his demise, he remained chairman of Tata Trusts, once again a position of great influence and power. However, despite being in these exalted corner offices, he never lost sight of being, first and foremost, a good human being. He was respectful of the people he worked with, he gave the highest priority to protecting their dignity and he was fixated with meeting every commitment he had made to people. Most importantly, he displayed care and compassion in ample measure when it was most required.

Pause for a moment and think of some of the different stories you have read in this book: how he responded to the 26/11 terror attacks at the Taj, how he would never raise his voice or lose his temper in public at any team member, or how he went out of his way to meet a commitment to doing a voice recording for a person he did not really know. Think of that simple question he asked N. Chandrasekaran, chairman of Tata Sons, when the renovation of Bombay House was being discussed: 'Where will the dogs go?' All these stories and so many others prove a very simple point—that Ratan Tata responded not just as a chairman, but as a human being. On so many occasions, it is this spontaneous yet deeply ingrained humanity that led Ratan to doing the right thing. Particularly in moments of intense crisis involving people, I would venture to say that his humanity shone through far more powerfully than his chairmanship.

There is a simple learning for each of us here. We should not get seduced by the positions of power that we may come to occupy, and thereby build walls around us. On the other hand, we must remember that we are, first and foremost, humans with heart and soul. Whether we are a senior executive in a plush corner office, or a successful entrepreneur who has built a unicorn or a zebra, or a top lawyer or doctor who is highly sought after, what will guide us to making the right decisions is the lens of humanity. Ratan Tata's life teaches us that being human in addition to being professional, particularly in situations where people are involved, enables us to strike the correct balance and take the right decisions.

To do this, we need to cultivate the human traits of respect, kindness, generosity, gratitude, empathy and care, and make them as important in our lives as the professional traits of developing sound strategy, ensuring excellent execution and staying focused on achieving results. This is what the life of Ratan Tata teaches us.

Refusing to Succumb

If there is one statement of Ratan Tata's that has stayed with me throughout the writing of this book, it is his satisfaction at going to bed every night 'knowing that I did not succumb'.

To do the right thing at all times, it is very important that we have this same principle on top of our minds: never to succumb to the many temptations that are likely to come our way, that threaten to derail us from the path of integrity or humanity.

Ratan Tata knew that despite choosing to live a life of integrity, or endeavouring to be totally true to his role as chairman of the Tata group, he would still be subject to temptation, as every human being is bound to be. This is even more true of any person in a position of power, because the world tends to throw a variety of enticements in their path to obtain what it requires from them. Therefore, I think, he specifically guarded against falling prey to these temptations.

This is such an important and timeless learning for each of us. If we aspire to do the right thing consistently in our lives and careers, it is important to bear in mind all the time that we are human beings who carry all the frailties and failings that humans are born with. Whatever role we occupy, however exalted, we are not gods and will never be. On the other hand, every professional, however senior or junior he or she is, is likely to be subject to the human temptations of short-term gratification, greed, lust, achieving results through unethical or questionable means, intellectual dishonesty and many other failings.

Therefore, constantly resolving never to succumb to these temptations is one of the best ways of ensuring that we do not fall prey to them.

A North Star

Through his obsession with doing the right thing, Ratan Tata has left behind learnings that each of us can make our own. Leading a life of integrity, embracing our roles, displaying humanity and refusing to succumb—these four principles appear to be simple no-brainers, but to practise them consistently requires a lot of willpower, moral fibre and stubborn determination.

Very importantly, on such challenging voyages, a guiding star always helps. Ratan Tata can be that role model, that Northern Star, to all of us who wish to do the right thing in our own lives.

And therefore I conclude this book with a small poetic flourish:

The stories of your life will light
Our quest to practise what is right
Bright, firm and clear from far
RNT, our Northern Star.

Epilogue

Looking Back, Looking Forward

I was appointed as brand custodian at Tata Sons by Ratan Tata, towards the end of October 2016. This also turned out to be my last full-time role with the Tata group. I retired from this role seven years later in December 2023, post my superannuation from the group.

I am, therefore, perhaps one of the few people who can claim with pride that Ratan Tata had a key role to play both in my recruitment to the group (he was a member of the Final Interview Board that selected me to the Tata Administrative Service, way back in 1987) and in my final full-time role in the group (which he assigned to me nearly thirty years later). This has made the writing of this book even more special for me.

My role as brand custodian also provided me the opportunity to work for the next several years with N.

Chandrasekaran (Chandra), who succeeded Ratan Tata as chairman of Tata Sons in February 2017.

I still have with me the statement that the board of Tata Sons released on 12 January 2017, announcing Chandra's appointment as chairman of Tata Sons. It said, 'Mr Chandrasekaran has demonstrated exemplary leadership as the chief executive officer and managing director of Tata Consultancy Services. We believe he will now inspire the entire Tata group to realize its potential acting as leaders in their respective businesses, always in keeping with our value system and ethics and adhering with the practices of the Tata group which have stood it in good stead.'

Ratan Tata, who had played a key role in the appointment of Chandra to this position, wrote a message congratulating Chandra soon after his appointment. This message reflected Ratan's confidence that the future of the group would be safe in Chandra's hands. Ratan's message read, 'I congratulate Chandra on his appointment as chairman of Tata Sons and the group. It is a well-deserved recognition of his proven leadership capabilities. The job is complex but I am sure he will take the group to new heights while protecting the group's values and ethics at all times.'

I had never earlier worked with Chandra, though I had met him on a few occasions during his stint as MD of Tata Consultancy Services (TCS). I knew him as a Tata lifer, who had led TCS on a voyage of rapid growth, increasing its market value by more than ten times during the eight years he served as managing director and CEO of the company. His single-minded focus on delivering world-class performance, and his outstanding leadership of business and people, were well known not just within the Tata group but across industry.

This focus became quite clear during Chandra's very first meeting with me, on the fourth floor of Bombay House. He understood my role as brand custodian and emphasized that whatever we do with respect to the Tata brand had to be world-class, without exception. 'We have to be the best,' he said, 'there can be no compromise on that.' Those words have resonated in my mind ever since. In many ways, they reminded me of the focus on excellence that Ratan Tata spoke about at several group events over the years.

During the seven years that I was a member of Chandra's leadership team at Tata Sons, I observed how this unrelenting focus on striving to be the best delivered superb results on so many fronts. As a result, under

Chandra's leadership, the value of the Tata brand grew rapidly from US$13.1 billion in 2017 to US$26.4 billion in 2023 (note : this is as per Brand Finance Global 500 reports). By 2025, the value of the Tata brand has increased even further, to US$31.6 billion. Throughout this period, Tata has maintained and strengthened its numero uno position in India, and has remained the only Indian origin brand amongst the top 100 most valuable brands in the world.

Ratan Tata led the creation of a unified identity for the Tata brand way back in the 1990s, and I think he would be very happy to see such remarkable growth in the value and global stature of the brand.

Even as I write this in 2025, it has been eight years since Chandra was appointed chairman of Tata Sons, and indeed he has taken the group to new heights during this period, as predicted by Ratan Tata. In his very first year in the role, Chandra spoke to many of us in the leadership team about the urgent need to simplify businesses, scale them and synergize across the group. Over the next few years, he urged businesses to get fit first and then set their sights on growing rapidly. This has resulted in most companies of the Tata group outpacing their competitors, and the group has improved its financial performance significantly. His focus on the need to prioritize consumer experience, sustainability, digital and AI across Tata companies has been relentless. Most importantly, through all these measures and more, he has guided companies of the group towards becoming fit and ready for the future.

In addition, Chandra has taken bold calls to invest in future-facing businesses that are important to India, thus taking forward the ethos of nation-building, which has been at the heart of the Tata group since the days of its founder, Jamsetji Tata. This has included large investments in the electronics and semiconductors industry, electric vehicles and batteries, driving unprecedented ambition in these new industries, which are so important to the nation's future.

This has also included the courageous decision to acquire Air India, thus bringing back home an airlines that had been created by the Tata group in 1932, but which had thereafter been nationalized by the Government of India in 1953. This acquisition was accompanied by a commitment to transforming Air India into a world-class airline that the nation can feel truly proud of.

So many of these ventures are driven by big dreams for India. Nation-building has been the mission of the Tata group ever since it was founded by Jamsetji Tata over

150 years ago, in 1868. Many decades later, J.R.D. Tata articulated this belief in his own words, that no material achievement is worthwhile unless it serves the needs or interests of the country and its people. Ratan Tata, throughout his tenure as chairman and until the end of his life, was constantly pursuing dreams for the development of India, as you have read in many of the stories in this book.

This is why I feel so proud of being part of the Tata group. That is why I am inspired to write books about the Tatas and their legendary leaders, including this one. I feel proud and inspired both as a Tata lifer and as an Indian. Because, I think, nothing can be more important than doing the right thing for our beloved nation.

* * *

Permit me to end this epilogue with an author's hope and also a writer's request.

My hope: I hope you have enjoyed reading this book and have found it useful. I hope many of the themes, thoughts, stories and quotes in these pages have inspired you.

My request: Please do provide me your views about this book. Feedback from readers like you is invaluable to authors like me.

My email address is bhatharish@hotmail.com.

Afterword

In the Words of Ratan Tata

I have had the privilege of listening to Ratan Tata speak on several occasions during my long career of more than thirty-five years with the Tata group. It was a privilege to hear him talk at various group events.

Some of these events, which I remember vividly, are the JRD-QV function held on J.R.D. Tata's birth anniversary (29 July) each year, and the Annual Group Management Meet of the Tata group where Ratan Tata would deliver a detailed chairman's address.

Ratan Tata always spoke thoughtfully and in a measured voice. When I listened to him, it was clear to me that he chose his words deliberately, after carefully thinking through their meaning and impact.

He has left behind with us a number of powerful and inspiring quotes, many of which are directly related to the theme of this book, perhaps because doing the right thing was always on top of his mind.

Here are fifteen of my favourite quotes from Ratan Tata, spanning many different themes relevant to our work and life. I hope these quotes inspire and guide you.

1. 'At all times, ask yourself if you are doing the right thing.'
2. 'A promise is a promise.'
3. 'Think big. Lead. Never follow.'
4. 'I would like to be remembered as a person who made a difference. Not anything more, not anything less.'
5. 'I view risk as an ability to be where no one has been before.'
6. 'The greatest pleasure I have had is trying to do something that everybody thought could not be done.'
7. 'Learn and listen because your whole world is going to be learning and listening.'
8. 'I can go to bed at night knowing that I did not succumb.'

9. 'One seems to learn much more during difficult times, so perhaps one should not be averse to them.'
10. 'India is still a developing country, one burdened with enormous disparities. It is our duty to play whatever role we can, in whichever way we can, to diminish those disparities.'
11. 'How many times have you heard people say this cannot be done? It is your job to remove these myths and get things done.'
12. 'If you speak or sit next to a Nobel laureate, he never tells you that he won a Nobel Prize. Other people tell you. So let humility be your best defence.'
13. 'If you can live with feeling happy about another company or another person's prosperity, then that would be the closest definition of happiness.'
14. 'The most valuable asset we have in our group is our ethical standards and our values.'
15. 'Our quest for quality, for excellence in business, should be never-ending. This is not a voyage where you can rest your oars.'

Acknowledgements

This book is inspired by Ratan Tata. I would like to acknowledge the deep impact he has had on my career and life.

Ratan Tata also provided me the opportunity to write my first book, *Tata Log*, thirteen years ago. I am ever thankful for that and there has been no looking back since then.

I would like to thank the Tata group for nurturing the author in me. The Tatas have been my professional home for nearly four decades now, and what a wonderful home this has been. Both my marketing studio and my writing table have stood firmly within this blue house.

My grateful thanks to N. Chandrasekaran, chairman, Tata Sons, for his consistent support and encouragement, and for his gracious words about this book, which I deeply value and cherish. He constantly urged me to pursue world-class excellence in everything I do, and I have borne this in mind throughout the writing of this book as well.

R. Gopalakrishnan, retired executive director of Tata Sons, and an accomplished author himself, has been my mentor on my writing voyage. I have also had the privilege of co-authoring a previous book with him. At my request, he reviewed the manuscript of this book closely, and provided me many valuable suggestions. Thank you, Sir.

Many of the stories in this book have emerged from my interviews with senior Tata professionals who reflected on their experiences with Ratan Tata, and gave generously of their effort and time. I would like to sincerely thank the following 'Tata Log' whose reflections and narrations have shaped this book.

Ishaat Hussain, Ravi Kant, B. Muthuraman, Kishore Chaukar, Donn Doongaji, Farokh Subedar, R.R. Bhinge, K.R.S. Jamwal, R. Mukundan, P.K. Ghose, Girish Wagh, H.N. Shrinivas, Bharat Vasani, Sidharth Sharma, Prabhat Pani and Lakshman Sethuraman.

I would also like to express my gratitude to Suhel Seth and Atul Bhide for sharing lovely anecdotes based on their interactions with Ratan Tata.

To my colleague Roopa Purushothaman, chief economist and head of policy advocacy at the Tata group, thank you for reading through the manuscript and for your excellent suggestions.

R.P. Narla, retired chief archivist of the Tata Central Archives and a good friend, also helped me greatly by reviewing this manuscript and providing me his perceptive comments.

The Tata Central Archives (TCA) has kindly provided me extensive source material and also some photographs for this book. TCA is a treasure trove of Tata documents, and I would like to compliment my colleagues there for how passionately they work on preserving Tata history.

For the wonderful photographs that are included in this book, I would like to convey sincere thanks to Tata Sons, Tata Business Excellence Group, Tata Steel, Tata Motors, Indian Hotels Company (IHCL), Shantanu Naidu and Atul Bhide.

I would like to acknowledge the many sources, including books and articles, which I have referred to during the writing of this book. These are detailed in the bibliography.

To Milee Ashwarya and the team at Penguin Random House India, thank you for being my constant partners on this voyage. My conversations with Milee have been very important in developing the themes and structure of this book. Her belief in my writing has been the wind under my wings. She has also been a hard taskmaster, though she cracks the whip with empathy.

Hitha Haridas, my editor on this book, has helped me in so many ways on this entire project. She never misses a single thing, and her expertise in editing the text, as well as on so many other matters relating to publishing a book, has been invaluable. Saloni Mital, managing editor at Penguin Random House, has helped shape the manuscript beautifully. Her command of the English language is amazing, and when she touches the raw text, she makes magic happen. My sincere thanks to both Hitha and Saloni.

To my mother, Jayanthi, and my mother-in-law, Vatsala, I thank them for their blessings. They are the elders of my family, and both of them take a keen interest in my writing. Both of them are also great admirers of Ratan Tata, and I look forward to gifting them the first two copies of this book.

My daughter, Gayatri, who now lives and works in Bangalore, has always been a constant source of encouragement on my writing journey. I have occasionally discussed this book with her, and I hope she likes the final product.

If this book has reached the finishing line and been published in 2025, a great deal of credit should go to my wife, Veena. She has monitored this project with a hawk's eye and has ensured that I do not get distracted with a million other things that keep flying up on my radar all the time. Her firm view (which she has expressed to me several times) is that her writer husband should, first and foremost, focus on his writing, and not make excuses for why this is not possible. She and I have also had countless discussions on many of the themes and stories in this book, and some arguments as well. Veena also took time to review the manuscript in detail and provided me many suggestions. Most importantly, her love, companionship and support have sustained me at every stage of the research and writing process.

I thank Goddess Saraswati for blessing me with the passion, capability, hunger and constant urge to write.

Writing has given me purpose when I wake up every morning, and fulfilment when I go to sleep at night. I am so happy that I am able to touch tens of thousands of minds and hearts through what I write. I hope and pray that I can continue to put this wonderful gift to the best possible use throughout my life.

Glossary

Here are a few acronyms and terms that are commonly used within the Tata group, and what they stand for. Many of these acronyms have been used in this book.

BEBP: Brand Equity and Business Promotion agreement

TCoC: Tata Code of Conduct

TBEM: Tata Business Excellence Model

OFI: Opportunities for Improvement (as thrown up by assessments under TBEM)

JRD-QV: JRD Quality Value Award (named after J.R.D. Tata)

TBExG: Tata Business Excellence Group

BRC: Business Review Committee

TCA: Tata Central Archives

TMTC: Tata Management Training Centre

IHCL:	Indian Hotels Company Limited
TPSWT:	Taj Public Service Welfare Trust
TCS:	Tata Consultancy Services
TCE:	Tata Consulting Engineers

Bibliography

Allen, Charles, and Sharda Dwivedi. *The Taj at Apollo Bunder*. Presentation by the Taj Mahal Palace Hotel. Mumbai: Pictor Publishing, 2010.

Bhat, Harish. *Tata Log*. New Delhi: Penguin India, 2012.

———. *#Tata Stories*. New Delhi: Penguin India, 2021.

Chacko, Philip, Christabelle Noronha, and Sujata Agrawal. *Small Wonder: The Making of the Nano*. New Delhi: Westland Ltd., 2010.

'Code of Honour.' Group Publications, Tata Sons. Chennai: Westland India, 2009.

'Business of Excellence.' Group Publications, Tata Sons, 2008.

Casey, Peter. *The Story of Tata: 1868 to 2001*. New Delhi: Penguin India, 2021.

Gupta, Deepali. *Tata vs Mistry: The Battle for India's Greatest Business Empire*. New Delhi: Juggernaut Books, 2019.

Irani, J.J. *Doctor Steel: My Life and Times with the Tatas*. New Delhi: Penguin India, 2023.

Kaw, M.K. *An Outsider Everywhere: Revelations by an Insider*. New Delhi: Konark Publishers, 2012.

Lala, R.M. *The Creation of Wealth*. New Delhi: Penguin India, 2004.

Mathew, Thomas. *Ratan Tata: A Life*. New Delhi: HarperCollins India, 2024.

Shah, Shashank. *The Tata Group: From Torchbearers to Trailblazers*. New Delhi: Penguin India, 2018.

Tata Review, Special Edition. Group Publications, Tata Sons, 2013.

Articles, Interviews and Other Features

Article on J.R.D. Tata., *Economic Times*, 26 March 1991.

'Changing India's Corporate Culture.' Interview by Ratan Tata. *Outlook*, global magazine of Andersen Consulting, January 2000.

'Ratan Tata's Absence Deeply Felt across the World, Writes PM Narendra Modi.' *The Hindu* (and other Indian newspapers), 9 November 2024.

'Tata Medical Centre: A Glorious Decade.' Booklet published by Tata Medical Centre. Kolkata, 2021.

'Walk the Talk with Ratan Tata.' Interview aired on NDTV, November 2010. https://www.ndtv.com.

Tata.com. The official website of the Tata Group.

Tatatrusts.org. The official website of the Tata Trusts.

Scan QR code to access the
Penguin Random House India website